The
Psychology
of
Wealth

The Psychology *of* Wealth

**Understand Your Relationship with
Money and Achieve Prosperity**

Charles Richards, Ph.D.

NEW YORK   CHICAGO   SAN FRANCISCO
LISBON   LONDON   MADRID   MEXICO CITY   MILAN
NEW DELHI   SAN JUAN   SEOUL   SINGAPORE
SYDNEY   TORONTO

The *McGraw-Hill* Companies

1 2 3 4 5 6 7 8 9 10   DOC/DOC   1 6 5 4 3 2 1

ISBN 978-0-07178929-5
MHID   0-07178929-4

e-book IBSN 978-0-07-178930-1
e-book MHID   0-07-178930-8

Interior design by Lee Fukui and Mauna Eichner

Library of Congress Cataloging-in-Publication Data

Richards, Charles L.
 The psychology of wealth : understand your relationship with money and achieve prosperity / by Charles Richards.
    p. cm.
 Includes index.
 ISBN-13: 978-0-07-178929-5 (alk. paper)
 ISBN-10: 0-07-178929-4 (alk. paper)
 1. Money—Psychological aspects. 2. Wealth—Psychological aspects. I. Title.
 HG222.3.R53 2012
 332.024'01--dc23
                        2011042545

McGraw-Hill books are available at special quantity discounts to use as premiums and sales promotions or for use in corporate training programs. To contact a representative, please e-mail us at bulksales@mcgraw-hill.com.

This book is printed on acid-free paper.

To my parents, Lewis Richards and Lydia H. Lockman,
and my grandparents, Guy and Rheba Hoffman,
who provided the foundation
on which I have been blessed to rely and build

Contents

Acknowledgments

When I set out to write this book, my intention was to help people develop a new way of thinking about prosperity and thereby improve their lives, even in the midst of an uncertain economy. In the process, I learned more than I could ever have anticipated. As I met and talked with dozens of people to uncover just what a psychology of wealth is, the richness of this topic unfolded. The knowledge, understanding, and inspiration that I gained through listening to their stories and gathering their insights are incalculable, and my gratitude is immense.

My most heartfelt gratitude goes to Katherine Hall, my senior editor, who led the editing and research team. She gave so much of herself and remained in love with the concept despite the long hours. Thanks also for the outstanding work of Sarah Martini, who shepherded the project with dedication and cheerful care. I owe much appreciation to Chris McKinley for his consultation and perspective on the history of finance. Christine Robinson and Teresa Rousch assisted skillfully with research and organization. Thank you to Rob Hall for his contribution to the cover design and to Aimee Hall for her organizational skill. John Scevola and his team provided essential marketing support. To all these gifted individuals, I am grateful.

Working with the McGraw-Hill Professional team has been a great experience. Special thanks to Senior Editor Donya Dickerson. My gratitude also goes to Gary Krebs, vice president and publisher; Mary Glenn, associate publisher; Ann Pryor, publicist; Zach Gajewski, development editor; Ruth W. Mannino, EDP manager; Sara Hendricksen, marketing manager; and Tom Lau, cover designer.

Many thanks to the folks at Planned Television Arts (PTA) for their savvy wisdom. David Hahn, PTA managing director, was a pivotal player in shaping the spirit of this book. Thank you, David, for helping to move this project in the right direction. I'd also like to offer special thanks to Jared Sharpe, director, PTA Finance and PTA Sports, and to Alexandra Kirsch, director, PTA Interactive.

Sarah Archer, who obtained many of the interviews recounted here, did a spectacular job of drawing out substantive details. Joseph "Bruno" Pelle was a quiet inspiration through the initial phases of our research efforts. My thanks to Sarah and Bruno, and to Dan Nyberg and Scott Olson for their artistry.

I was privileged to have private interviews with two of the most brilliant finance minds in America: Dr. Harold Black and Dr. Frederick Miller. My gratitude goes to them and to Marcia Miller, Jeff Burch, Erin Wagner, and Lori Mabry.

Some of the most moving stories I have recounted in these pages are those of Senator Leticia Van de Putte, Representative Johnny Shaw, Dennis Gardin, Joey Wincek, Dr. Rickie Keys, and Tony and Mike Cupisz. From challenging beginnings, these courageous people have created superb lives and have helped others do the same. I thank each of them for having taught me through example about the psychology of wealth.

Wholehearted thanks to everyone whose personal stories and insights contributed to my understanding of the psychology of abundance and who made me feel wealthier for the experience: former U.S. Representative J. C. Watts, Dr. Michael Stern, Lennie Alzate, Bennie Taylor, Jane Pulkys, Denise Fast, Bill and Deb Mann, Peachie Bailey, Anne Norton, Sammy Kicklighter, Joyce Shirley, and Libby Fine. To honor their privacy, others are identified in these pages by first name only. I thank them all.

There are people who simply stand out for their achievements. A special thanks to Donald J. Trump, and to Stuart Johnson and Darren Hardy of *SUCCESS* magazine, for their inspirational work and their dedication to helping others find success. Thanks also to Leah McCann of the SUCCESS Foundation.

This book wouldn't have come into being without Alden Butcher and Anne Archer. Their insights are found on virtually every page, and I could not have brought this book to fruition without them. Alden's creative talents, patience, and wisdom are always very much appreciated. Thanks to both of you for your unfailing friendship, encouragement, and vision.

In addition, I would like to honor my friends, who have provided unconditional caring and kindness at all times, including Barbara King, Matthew and Deborah Mitchell, Jay Hare, Dr. Michael Stern, Christina Chomut, Harold Ware, Tunde Baiyewu, Divina Infusino, Brian and Arielle Ford, Doc Lew Childre, Deborah Rozman, Lisa Nelson, Linda Anderson, and many others. And, as always, a special thanks for the support and inspiration of Joan and Harold Klemp.

Golden Steps

Whatever you think you can do, or believe you can do, begin it. Action has magic, grace and power in it.

—Johann Wolfgang von Goethe

In my many years as a practicing psychotherapist, I have met, counseled, and learned from people in a wide variety of financial situations. Through listening to people from affluent executives who live like pashas to workers who live from paycheck to paycheck, I have been privy to the cares, woes, and joys of having and not having much money.

As an executive coach and trainer, I have worked with many well-to-do clients, some of whom simply are not comfortable in their financial skin. Their relationship with money is fraught with the fear that their riches may disappear or that they will be exposed as impostors. Before I worked with these people, I had assumed that it was perfectly natural for people with meager financial resources to worry about money. But why were these well-off individuals not feeling the psychological benefits of their enviable position? And what about my associates and friends with very modest means who were confident, happy, and secure about their finances? These fortunate souls seemed to share a sense of comfort and control in their relationships with money.

In short, they led rich and rewarding lives without having many "riches" in the conventional sense.

I wondered: What's the difference? Why do people of many different financial stripes feel a perpetual state of lack and fear about money, while others, also found across a wide spectrum of financial situations, feel genuinely prosperous? In short, why do some people possess what I had come to see as a *psychology* of wealth, no matter how financially wealthy they may or may not be? I also wondered whether deeper traits or habits are common to this psychology of abundance and whether they can be learned. What can people who have created lives of a more encompassing wealth teach us, if anything?

I had been casually pondering these questions when the economic crisis hit in 2008. Against the backdrop of a faltering national and global economy, my questions about financial confidence and empowerment became more pressing. Like many people, I was troubled by the state of the economy and its impact on my neighbors' lives. I was concerned about the implications of runaway debt, the loss of so many homes and jobs, and the collapse of trust in our financial institutions. Suddenly, what had looked like the perfect environment in which to gain wealth and to create a better life was being exposed as a house of cards.

As a citizen, I wanted to know: how did we get into this mess? And as a psychotherapist, I wanted to discover: how might we, as individuals, get out of it? How could we climb out of the frightening morass of poor choices and gloomy prospects that, in many ways, seemed to be beyond our control? At least part of the answer seemed to lie in understanding our individual and collective psychology concerning finances. And so I considered what more I could learn about a psychology of wealth that would help answer these questions—that is, how did we get here, and how could we move ahead with more hope and confidence?

I began to investigate this psychology in earnest. I started reading, and I started seeking out people who displayed a healthy relationship with money. I wanted to find out what they know about prosperity that many of us do not. How do they think, and what do they do differently? I interviewed people who seemed either to intrinsically possess a psychology of wealth or to have acquired one. I also spoke with finance professors, legislators, consultants, and credit counselors. I traveled to seminars and attended press conferences, where I listened to people who have been affected by the economic downturn. I talked with owners of booming international businesses, people with limited resources who have created balanced lives, and people who dedicate their days to nonprofit organizations and feel prosperous in their personal choices. In other words, I looked for people who I felt might hold a clue. Their wisdom and stories are the heart of this book.

From these stories, a picture of a wealth psychology began to emerge. In it I saw fascinating elements of self-esteem, responsibility, risk taking, achievement, and determination. I also learned how people with a wealth psychology deal with obstacles and setbacks. I observed how they approach giving to others from a sense of gratitude and also intuitively sense that giving is part of their own forward momentum. And in the stories of folks who either choose or are forced to restart their lives, I found heartening lessons about the near-infinite capacity of human beings to adapt and thrive.

One aspect of the global economic crisis that continues to play a central role for both individuals and the economy is debt. Debt is getting a great deal of press and is at the forefront of many discussions; the subject stirs both argument and anxiety. I knew that looking at debt would be key to understanding a psychology of wealth. Among the most unexpected things I learned is that, while debt has recently been the undoing of some homeowners and consumers, many people who use credit regularly are not in trouble. On the contrary, I learned about ways of borrowing that are helping people move ahead, both materially and psychologically. And so I dug deeper. I learned that debt, while much maligned, has actually been a major engine of growth, progress, and prosperity throughout history. For both individuals and the economy, debt, when used wisely, has been, and can be, a good thing.

What appears to have gotten us into trouble, both individually and collectively, is behaving unconsciously. In many ways, we have fallen into a kind of inattentiveness in our borrowing and spending, unhitching these activities from broader goals, achievement, and genuine advancement. Perhaps not surprisingly, in people with a healthy psychology of wealth, I found habits of spending, borrowing, and—most important—living consciously. It is these habits of consciousness that seem to hold the secret to turning even the most limiting circumstances into psychological and material gold.

Today there is vigorous public debate about how we should and shouldn't spend, invest, save, and borrow. Financial advisors, economists, and entire governments take positions on how we should use our money. In writing this book, I have tried not to add another financial strategy to the conversation, but instead to share answers to the question of what it takes to create an inner sense of abundance and meaning in our financial lives. These answers provide tremendous optimism about our prospects. The people whose stories are gathered here have a great deal to tell us about how we can prosper and achieve wealth in the fullest sense of the word.

As Goethe said, "Action has magic, grace and power in it." Creating our own stories begins with action—with the small steps and seemingly small choices that we make each day. Once you begin, each step can be golden, and the next step is right in front of you.

How Do We Define Wealth?

Don't ask yourself what the world needs;
ask yourself what makes you come alive.
And then go and do that. Because what the
world needs is people who have come alive.

—Harold Thurman Whitman

It was yet another beautiful day in the barrio of San Antonio, Texas, where Leticia San Miguel grew up. Her Mexican American family had lived here for 200 years, and her roots ran deep. The family had been on this land when it was part of Spain, France, Mexico, the Republic of Texas, the Southern Confederacy, and now the United States. The name of the area had changed, but the people had not. The culture was old and rich, if not wealthy. Leticia's family and friends all lived within a few blocks of one another. Cousins were like brothers and sisters. Family, church, and community—these were the essence of the barrio. Yet somehow Leticia acquired a mindset of wealth—an uncommon strength and drive. She was to reveal a powerful belief in her own intrinsic value and her capacity to achieve.

Politics had never been Leticia's goal. She had wanted to follow in the footsteps of her grandfather, who had been a pharmacist.

After her marriage, as a young adult, she took a chance and bought her own pharmacy. "It was my dream, but it was risky. We used everything we had saved for buying a new home. I grew that pharmacy into a medical center in a very underserved area of San Antonio." At the same time, Leticia was building her family. She laughs, "I had six children in ten years. We were running two businesses. I would take my baby to work with me. My patients would sit in the rocking chair and rock her."

A psychology of wealth can be learned in childhood through the values we are taught—not just from the size of our home or the neighborhood we live in. These values are about achievement, inner strength, and belief in oneself. Leticia recounts pivotal lessons that she learned from her dad. "When I was introduced to adults and they would say, 'What a pretty little girl,' my dad would respond, 'She's the first in her class.' It gave me the message: it's not how you look; it's what's in your brain. My father knew the power of words. I did not have a Barbie doll figure. My dad turned that into a strength by encouraging me to participate in track. He taught me that it's not how you look; it's how strong you are."

Leticia speaks proudly of her mother, too. "From my mother came a different perspective. There was never a question of whether I would go to college. My parents were the first in their families to do so; they broke that barrier. My mom always said you have to have your degree and a career, so you can live a life of dignity, both for yourself and for your children. She said I would be defined by that.

"My grandmother was also important in my life. She taught me a lesson through her actions. She created a little business that we called the Ice House. People bought ice there, but also tacos and drinks, and on the weekends there was music and dancing under the trees by the picnic tables. She used a loan to get her business started and later to build an addition on her house. I would go with her into town to pay the bill. We'd go to Eagle Loan to pay her monthly installment payment and then to the soda fountain. It was an adventure, but I understood the lesson: 'You pay your debts, and you are responsible.' Doing that with her every month helped me establish a good relationship with money."

Then Leticia asks, "Now, why did she need to borrow money to expand her home? Some would have said that, at her advanced age, it was impractical. But when she later became ill, that addition allowed her to be at home and keep her dignity. Somehow she knew what was right for her."

The willingness to accept responsibility for one's own life is the source from which self-respect springs.

—Joan Didion

You're a Girl

A defining incident in Leticia's life occurred when she was in the eighth grade. "The boys were trying to decide who should run for student council offices. I was a member of the council, and I said, 'Well, I could run.' The boys said, 'No, you can't run.' I asked, 'Why not?' They answered, 'Because you're a girl.' That was the first time anyone had ever said I couldn't do something because I was a girl, and it strengthened my resolve. I said, 'Watch me. I can do this.' It was the first time I was assertive. No girl had ever been student council president. I campaigned and took a chance on myself." And Leticia won.

"When I grew up," she says, "I was plenty busy as a small business owner and a mother of six. But I was very active in my community. When a seat in the Texas House of Representatives became available, I realized that no candidates were discussing what I thought were the important issues. My husband said, 'Why don't you run for state rep?' I answered, 'Because I couldn't win.' At the time there were 150 state legislators, but only about a dozen of them were women. He said, 'No, baby, you'll win.' So we had a family meeting. We wanted to see what the kids thought about the possibility that I would be away part of the time. The little one asked, 'Why does Mommy want to be a state *'epsenative*?' My 10-year-old daughter answered, 'Because there are not enough mommies there.' My husband and I looked at each other in shock. We both knew I had to do this."

Again, Leticia won. After five terms as a state representative, today Leticia is known as Senator Van de Putte and is serving her fifth term in the Texas Senate.[1] She is a political and moral force to be reckoned with, representing the 880,000 people in her district, more constituents than in a federal congressional district.

Leticia explains: "Representing the people of my district is one of the most intensely satisfying things I've ever done. And I've encouraged leadership in my kids and grandkids: to be decision makers and become involved. I am very optimistic. I am not a doom-and-gloom person. What jazzes me is that this generation of kids may be the greatest generation ever. We just have to keep things together enough so this generation has the opportunity to become leaders."

What allowed Leticia to achieve such remarkable success in a career dominated by men? Like many of the successful people I have known and worked with in my practice as a psychotherapist, Leticia was willing to bet on herself. Just as important, she believed that through her efforts and focus, she could reach her goal. She had grown up knowing that she could accomplish what she set out to do. And with each achievement, her sense of confidence, prosperity, and self-worth expanded.

None of her success was built on a foundation of financial wealth. It was Leticia's sense of her own intrinsic worth that propelled her to achieve her goals. If she had accepted other people's expectations, she wouldn't have even tried to run for president of the student council or for the Texas legislature. Instead, she had the psychology of someone who belonged in a position of responsibility and power. She stretched, and she won the bet. She invested in herself, and it paid off. She was taught, "Try hard, no matter what. Not trying is the failure."

When asked how she defines wealth, Leticia is philosophical: "At the end of my time here, I want to have lived a life of significance, to know that I was not a taker, that my life has meant something to my family and my community. Have I done something to improve the lives of others? How I answer that question is what defines a rich and rewarding life for me."

An Inherent Worth

Luckily for most of us, being wealthy is *not* a requirement for developing either a sense of self-worth or a psychology of wealth. What Leticia's story teaches us is that success does not require a great deal of money; what it requires is a belief in one's inherent worth and a willingness to make a conscious investment in oneself—even if that means taking a certain amount of risk. To achieve anything worthwhile requires that we take some chances and be willing to move out of our comfort zone. This doesn't mean betting the farm; not every risk will pan out. But I've learned that people who achieve true prosperity let neither risk nor setbacks stop them. They don't give in or give up on themselves. If one approach doesn't work, they will try another. They know that if they are to be the hero of their own lives, they must be willing to take whatever steps will move them toward their dreams and their goals.

MONEY AS CURRENCY

It's no coincidence that money is also called currency, taken from the word *current*—the flow of electric charge through a conductor. To survive and thrive, we must learn to act as better conductors of currency. Currency represents energy expended in some form of work. This work can be expressed as physical labor, in the creative arts, or as specialized knowledge in science, law, engineering, or finance. Learning to manage money responsibly and serve others is like being able to use electric current in a productive manner. We can become powerful transformers for the currency of society. How we use that power is a great responsibility.

How We Learn a Wealth Psychology

Just as a computer has an operating system, every family operates according to a set of spoken and unspoken rules. I call this the *family operating system*. This system greatly influences an individual's thinking and behavior. In the never-finished "nature vs. nurture" debate, research shows that nature, as expressed in each person's genotype, has the upper hand in defining one's biological uniqueness. However, in the formation of a personal psychology, the ways in which one is—or isn't—nurtured are powerful factors in molding what nature has provided. As a result, the family operating system may strongly influence how an individual thinks and behaves.

Your family operating system effectively helps to program your beliefs, attitudes, skills, anxieties, and expectations, both conscious and unconscious. In addition to the programming you receive from your family, your mindset is also colored by your early schooling and the general environment in which you were raised. This operating system specifically affects your attitudes and beliefs about money, wealth, and financial success. The programming you receive can greatly condition—for better or worse—the degree of monetary gain or financial wealth that you are likely to achieve. Examining your background and the family operating system that you were exposed to is an important step in making constructive changes in your subconscious programming about money, wealth, and prosperity.

But if you didn't learn a psychology of wealth from your family, can you still learn it? Can you gain the attitude and habits that drive success? Most certainly. That's a simple answer, yet indeed many people can and do prosper financially despite being raised with meager resources or a lack of family support. And, of course, the converse is true: many people who were raised in wealth fail miserably with every opportunity; even with encouragement and resources, they do not seem to achieve their greatest potential. A psychology that includes balanced and empowered attitudes about money and self can be learned in a family with either vast or very modest means—or it can be learned on one's own.

Indeed, Leticia's story is one of many that tell about people from humble beginnings who have achieved a rich and rewarding life. Like Leticia, they seem to carry within them a sense of abundance that manifests itself in success, regardless of their financial origins. A story that is now familiar to many of us begins with an idealistic young father who nonetheless abandoned his wife and his baby son, forcing them to live with relatives in very modest circumstances. When the boy was six, his mother remarried, effectively uprooting the family again—this time moving to a distant and unfamiliar country. Within several years, that marriage also failed, and the mother, the boy, and now a baby sister retreated to their relatives' home again. When the boy was in his teens, his mother again left the United States, this time alone, to pursue her career. By now you may recognize this boy as Barack Obama, the first African American president of the United States.

In spite of coming from a broken home with little stability and meager financial resources, young Obama had a mother who doted on him and loved him dearly. She and his grandparents instilled in him a belief in his own abilities, laying the foundation for him to reach his full potential. His mother expected great things of him. And she helped him become responsible for his own progress in life, awakening him before dawn every day to home-school him before his regular school day began. Barack Obama's story is one of many that illustrate the concept that a true psychology of wealth is not based solely on one's financial status, circumstances, or resources. Personal values regarding success, motivation, and self-confidence can be the building blocks for a psychology of wealth.

Unfortunately, the principles of a learned psychology of wealth, which include self-worth and one's relationship with money, can also work to one's detriment. If you are born into a family whose mindset is that of financial failure or victimhood, then a healthy sense of self-worth and a sound psychology of wealth can be much harder to come by.

I Won the Lottery!

Some curious examples of how this lack of a psychology of wealth can allow even the rich to fail are found in stories of people who win the lottery. All too often, their lives unravel when the money floods in. They quickly lose not only their bearings, but often their millions. It's a short trip from "I won the lottery!" to failure. The problem is not only that the sudden winners are unschooled in how to handle money; often their very identities crumble as the expectations and attitudes of their friends, family members, and others shift suddenly and dramatically.

That situation is exactly the one that Shefik Tallmadge found himself in at the age of 29. In 1988, Tallmadge won what at that time was the largest jackpot ever in the Arizona lottery: $6.7 million, or $335,000 each year for 20 years. Eventually he lost every penny. Tallmadge later acknowledged, "They gave me enough money to get into trouble, but not enough money to make me rich. I made some mistakes—very, very expensive mistakes." Unfortunately, having more money most likely would not have helped him. When people lack a healthy psychology of wealth, the decisions that cause them to lose $6.7 million are the same kinds of decisions that will cause them to founder no matter what amount of money is involved.

According to Shanna Hogan of *Times Publications*, when Tallmadge walked into a convenience store to pick up a bite to eat and check his weekly lottery ticket, he had just a few dollars left to see him through the next two weeks until his next paycheck. She described the scene: "The clerk routinely inserts the ticket into the machine to see if it's a winner. The machine immediately begins playing a happy tune. 'You can't cash this here. You have to go to Phoenix,' the clerk tells him as he hands back the ticket. 'All the numbers match.' 'What?' Tallmadge says in disbelief, examining the ticket."[2]

Tallmadge was a winner, but not for long. He wasted no time starting to spend. Upon receiving his first check, he quit working. Next, he went shopping and bought a new Porsche 911 Carrera convertible and a Rolex. Then he took his immediate family on a trip around the world. Afterward, Tallmadge enrolled in Northern Arizona University, where he met his wife.

Sometime after graduation, he and his wife moved to California, where they bought several houses, including one on the beach. Tallmadge's first problems involved California income taxes, so he and his wife moved to Florida, which has no state income tax. There they bought two more beach houses. Tallmadge had also experienced one of the common drawbacks of suddenly coming into a large amount of money—a deluge of people asking for help. For Tallmadge, the requests from friends, family members, and even total strangers had started within hours. In addition, he was the prey of companies that were constantly pressuring him to exchange his annual lottery payments for a lump-sum payment at 40 cents on the dollar. He eventually gave in and took one of these lump-sum payments. With that money, he invested in several gas stations, which soon failed.

In 2005, while battling with the IRS over back taxes, Tallmadge filed for bankruptcy. The *Arizona Republic* quoted him as saying, "I entered into the big shark pool, and I was the little minnow. The lottery did change my life. What I did with it afterward was the problem."[3] His wife is now the main breadwinner in the Tallmadge family, and he is a stay-at-home dad.

According to the Certified Financial Planner Board of Standards, nearly one-third of all lottery winners end up losing it all.[4] So, what are the other two-thirds doing right? Milt Laird, of Paso Robles, California, is one of the success stories—and he has insight into the reasons that his experience differed from that of so many others. David Fusaro of the Columbia News Service wrote of Laird's experience, "He won a $27 million jackpot in the California lottery in 1990 and has been comfortably retired on his California vineyard ever since." Laird and his wife used their windfall to travel and to make smart investments and consciously considered their donations to charities, family, and friends. Laird explains what made the difference in their lottery success: having a sturdy emotional foundation before winning the lottery was the key to their happiness. "'I think a lot of people are unhappy with their life for various reasons,' he said. 'They attribute it to a lack of money; then they get money and they think everything is going to be perfect.'"[5] In other words, Laird's healthy relationship with money allowed him to maintain his balance and use his financial boon to create a truly prosperous life.

The Magnolia Housing Project

Rickie Keys grew up in the Magnolia Housing Project in New Orleans in the 1970s. Despite its beautiful name, Magnolia had more murders per capita than any other housing project in the city. The number of violent crimes committed there was higher than that in many entire municipalities elsewhere in the United States. Murder, pimping, assault, and larceny were common occupations.

Rickie got out. He borrowed money to go to college, graduated from Tulane University, and later earned a Ph.D. As founder and president of Renewal Financial Services,[6] based in Shreveport, Louisiana, he is sought out for his plainspoken, no-nonsense financial advice. He works with financial services companies around the United States, helping people who are underserved by traditional banks with financial education and budget-skills training. Rickie enjoys a richly rewarding life, and he's teaching others to do the same. Considering where he came from, this is no small feat. In an obvious understatement, Rickie says, "People in my neighborhood didn't have resources." Yet he was able to navigate out of circumstances that resembled shark-infested waters.

Rickie says with pride, "Gloria Mae Keys, my mom, was a strict disciplinarian. She knew what we had to do to get out of our situation. Having faith and getting an education were two of the most important steps. Everything about money that I believe to be important I learned from my mother. She sat us down at the kitchen table and taught us what her father taught her: 'kitchen-table economics.' You can have either a good relationship or a bad relationship with money. And my relationship with money is good. It's like any relationship: there are ways to make it work. The rules are simple. You take responsibility. You budget. You pay in cash or charge things and pay them off. You take care of yourself and maintain balance. Don't spend more than you take in. Put some away for a rainy day, and invest where you can."

Rickie finds the roots of his inspiration in his family's past. "Certainly my mother was my greatest inspiration, and she taught me well. But I had no role model for monetary success," he says. "I didn't know what it looked like. So I took the street-cars up and down St. Charles Avenue in New Orleans. Through the windows, I watched the antebellum mansions go by—large homes, cars, and beautiful lawns. Those images stuck with me and gave me something to strive for. I also sought out people I admired."

One of those people was Rickie's grandfather. Despite bitter poverty, Joseph Colbert had achieved prosperity. Rickie explained, "My granddaddy owned 68 acres of land in Louisiana.

He started out as a sharecropper on a plantation and was encouraged to buy acreage. He was inspired by others around him who were more successful. He didn't have the money to buy the land and build a house, so he paid for the farm in installments. One of my aunts told me that, although the children had to help work the land, he made sure they all went to school. She said, 'We didn't know how blessed we were. But we learned that you can have what you want. You just have to work for it.'

"My granddaddy taught his children well. They all had the opportunity to go to college, and five of them did. Several received master's degrees. He taught them about money. My aunt also remembers some of his kitchen-table lessons: 'Don't spend it all. Use it wisely.' And my favorite: 'Always put up a dry stick for a wet day.' My granddaddy promised us that the farm would always stay a part of the family, and it has. With 12 children, he did not have much to leave except that land, but he also bestowed a vision of independence and prosperity. As a young kid, living in one of the worst inner-city environments imaginable, I held that vision in my heart. It is a part of who I am. I respected his accomplishments. I realized what it meant—that I could do it, too."

The reason man may become the master of his own destiny is because he has the power to influence his own subconscious mind.   —Napoleon Hill

---

The Fortunate Few

If you, like Dr. Rickie Keys and Senator Leticia Van de Putte, are among the fortunate few, you may have been born into a family or household whose outlook on wealth and money transcends the conventional perspective on prosperity. This way of thinking and being may have little to do with monetary status, financial advantages, or family wealth. It may be a deep-seated knowledge that you belong to a family that loves you, or a strong sense that your work makes a positive difference in the world. It could be a quiet confidence in your ability to achieve your dreams, no matter what life brings, or it may be a feeling of inner peace. If so, your birthright is much more valuable than any amount of money. In such a family, you would have had the opportunity to see that wealth is more than an accounting of financial assets.

Countless authors, philosophers, and academics have pondered the meaning of wealth. New books and articles telling stories of personal and financial triumph over challenging circumstances are published almost daily. Volumes of financial advice and "how to get rich" formulas are written by successful people from all walks of life. Yet in spite of this abundant guidance, many of us never achieve the kind of wealth we desire. In part, this is because a single definition of wealth—and therefore, a magic formula for achieving it—simply doesn't exist. When it comes to financial success, one size does not fit all.

While many of the stories we read on this topic are inspiring and meaningful, no single story can take into account the unique circumstances and decisions that each of us face at any given moment in our lives. On television, we currently are hearing popular financial advisors counsel us to save every possible penny and cut out all luxuries, even family vacations. This broad-brush approach overlooks individual values and circumstances that can make all the difference.

For example, these advisors may question why a couple with limited resources would decide to take their kids to Disneyland. Yet a closer look could reveal special circumstances, such as an illness in the family, that give the trip significance and value that can't be readily seen by someone outside the family. What if a child is so inspired by the experience that she decides to work toward becoming a cartoonist for Disney? This, in fact, is exactly what happened with the son of a good friend of mine. The boy even went on to surpass his childhood ambition to become a Disney animator and today is a successful movie producer. Although the vacation expenditure may seem to yield no immediate, tangible, or practical result, its value for the family may be incalculable, and that is not something we can judge for others. Like Leticia's grandmother, we must have the freedom to pave our own way, make our own decisions, and let our life be of our own making.

What is important to one individual is frivolous to another. The sheer diversity of human beings—of our circumstances, backgrounds, needs, and desires—makes a single approach to finances and a single definition of wealth not only out of reach but meaningless. One person's indulgence is another's essential component of a good life—and neither is right nor wrong. The diversity simply reflects the impact of individual perspectives on the meaning of prosperity and how each of us relates to money. We must define what wealth means to us, based on where we are, where we've come from, and where we want to go.

A psychology of wealth can evolve through either absorbing the values of our family or community or, if those values are antithetical to us, rejecting the early influences of our youth entirely. The latter scenario provides some of the most dramatic examples of an individual's power to create and define a prosperous life.

Poor Is a State of Mind

If you met Tony Cupisz, you might think he was born with a silver spoon in his mouth. He appears fit and tanned, and he wears well-cut suits. He has a kind of natural, youthful exuberance that is magnetic. I met him backstage as he was about to speak to 20,000 associates from his company, who were cheering with excitement. Tony is a cofounder of an international company that offers telecommunications and other services through independent business owners all over the world. He and his partners started the company in a competitive market with little support. Their organization is now heading toward a billion dollars in annual revenue; as of 2011, it was one of the largest direct sellers of telecommunications and essential home services in the world.

In the process of growing their business, Tony and his brother Mike, along with their two partners, have created the opportunity for tens of thousands of people to participate in their success. Many of these people now have prosperity stories of their own to share. As part of the audience, I had listened to some of these remarkable accounts before I went backstage to meet Tony. It was impressive to listen to such a diverse collection of successful and highly motivated people. It had made me even more curious about the men who had built such an exceptional company. When I found Tony backstage, the affection and respect that his colleagues had for him was apparent. He was surrounded by his company's top sales representatives, each of whom wanted a few minutes of his advice and encouragement. His generosity was obvious as, with a smile, he gave each person his full attention. He was clearly in his element. With a wink and a wave, he walked onstage.

Tony's childhood was challenging. He and his twin brother Mike don't really talk about it much, if ever. What they experienced is very much in the past. But the sharp contrast between their tough childhood and their brilliant success as adults begs for an explanation. When Tony later shared his story privately, what struck me most was his emphasis on gratitude. He explains it this way: "To me, happiness and wealth is being completely, 100 percent grateful for anything good that you have—and then building on that. That's where you start. Because I think everybody has something good in their lives. Life often doesn't seem fair, but we can all start with that attitude and find what we are grateful for."

He says, "As a kid, although we didn't have much money, I didn't know what 'poor' was, because poor is a state of mind as well as a financial condition, if you know what I mean. A very wealthy, sophisticated person might go bankrupt, but you wouldn't look at a person like that and say they're poor. There's poor, and then there's just no money. Your perceptions and beliefs matter. Success is achievable if you choose it and work at it. But if you don't choose it or believe it, you most likely will not have success. You really have to work on yourself—on your attitude, and your beliefs, and the way you think.

"You have to believe it's possible—and do something. Not everybody ends up doing exactly what they thought they would. But sometimes they end up doing things that are great, simply because they took a step that made them aware of something they could do."

Tony also talked about doing everything you can to move ahead in life. He believes that success comes from making good choices. Everyone will face obstacles, he said, but if you want to experience prosperity, you have to keep moving ahead doing something—and do it with passion. That's what he's doing.

Over the years, I've coached senior executives whose accomplishments are reflected in their sky-high salaries and luxurious lifestyles. Some of these highly successful people admit that they love their jobs so much that, if necessary, they'd do them for nothing. Like Tony, they are grateful and consider themselves blessed to have fulfilling work. However, others, including top executives in Fortune 100 corporations, live with relentless anxiety. They are driven by the fear that someday, somehow, they might lose everything; a few even fear becoming homeless. Clearly these two sets of apparently successful individuals have developed different views of wealth, success, and prosperity— and their relationship to them.

For truly successful people like Tony Cupisz, however, wealth cannot be defined strictly in terms of finances. "The real things in life that people want are so much more than money," Tony asserts. "There are people who are wealthy in family, or wealthy in love, or wealthy in friendship. Others have great health. You could have money and not have friends or family or love or good health in your life. To me, wealth is having what you really want in life. I have a friend who has a great family. He makes decent money, but he is very rich in his family. He has a great wife; he has twin daughters; he has two great sons. You couldn't buy what he has with any amount of money. The really important things you simply can't buy."

Understand Your Relationship with Money to Create Prosperity

If you were to define the word *wealth* right now, which words would you use? Everyone may define this word slightly differently, but most likely your definition of wealth encompasses abundance. And if you are like most of us, that means financial abundance. It's no wonder. A look in Merriam-Webster's dictionary shows that wealth can be defined as an "abundance of valuable material possessions or resources."

The way you answer this simple question about the definition of wealth can help to reveal your conscious view of money and success. Discovering the *unconscious* attitudes and concepts that may be driving you may take more work. Having a clear understanding of your own attitudes and desires—both conscious and unconscious—is a good place to start on your journey to a healthy relationship with abundance. By examining and identifying your concepts of success, career, work, and achievement, you can begin to break limiting patterns and unlock your own potential to achieve true prosperity.

Socrates understood a concept that remains relevant today: "The unexamined life is not worth living." By making the effort to consider where we stand in life and where we want to go, we can begin to evolve and move forward. If we do not examine both the conscious and the subconscious beliefs that drive us, life can become an endless pattern of unconscious repetition. Through examination and contemplation of our deepest beliefs and influences, however, we can break an unhealthy cycle and move forward.

What concepts and attitudes about money and wealth have you learned from your parents, your community, and your culture? Certainly your upbringing and early environment will have helped to shape your view of yourself and your attitudes toward money and success. But that does not mean that we are locked into the psychology of wealth—or the lack thereof—that we learned as children. Through the examples of courageous clients I have seen in my practice and the many people I've met while writing this book, I have discovered that it is seldom too late to grow and to learn new ways of thinking and being. Opportunities to change our course and set our sights on new horizons never end. To begin, we must examine where we are on the continuum of success, wealth, happiness, and health.

What Does It Take?

I couldn't embark on an investigation of the psychology of wealth without considering the "law of attraction," a concept that burst into the national spotlight after the movie *The Secret* was released in 2006. *The Secret* inspired an enormous wave of interest, controversy, and questions. Why?

The movie's core message is "like attracts like." That is, positive thinking brings about positive results, and negative thinking leads to negative results. For example, by making a positive statement, such as "I am rich," you can create the reality of financial success. The reason for the movie's popularity is no mystery: it promises that we can take control of our lives and create wealth through the power of imagination and intention. Predictably, its claims about the effectiveness of positive thinking brought a critical backlash. Yet the ideas behind it are at least as old as the Bible, with its wise assertion that with a little faith, nothing is impossible—even the movement of the proverbial mountain. These ideas are also based in some science.

I truly admire the work of Bruce Lipton, Ph.D. This famed cellular biologist and recipient of the Goi Peace Award is the author of *The Biology of Belief: Unleashing the Power of Consciousness, Matter, and Miracles.* Bruce has demonstrated that our thoughts have the power to heal or harm us and that we can even change our bodies at a cellular level by retraining our thinking. He observes that "70 percent or more of our thoughts . . . are negative and redundant," and therefore we may be doing ourselves harm by not paying attention to what we think. As Bruce and I discussed at a recent workshop that he and Robert M. Williams co-facilitate each year, positive thinking is just the beginning. Bruce often cites Rob Williams's work as offering effective approaches to altering consciousness and effecting positive change.[7] In my own life, I have also appreciated the simplicity of Rob's methods to expedite inner and outer changes. Whatever method one may use, a new state of mind must be put into practice in order to move forward in life and achieve something greater.

> *Your current thoughts are creating your future life. What you think about the most or focus on the most will appear as your life.*   —Rhonda Byrne

The Secret raised interesting questions about the role of consciousness in the psychology of wealth. It encourages us to ask: what internal changes are required to develop a psychology of wealth? And what are you really striving for when you strive for a prosperous life? To answer these questions, it helps to understand not only your own psychology and family history, but the "family history" of wealth itself. In the next chapter, we will enter wealth's attic and unpack the family album of its journey in America to start discovering how we can join its rich evolution.

The Evolution
of Wealth

*Almost everybody today believes that
nothing in economic history has ever
moved as fast as, or had a greater impact
than, the Information Revolution.
But the Industrial Revolution moved at
least as fast in the same time span, and
had probably an equal impact if not a
greater one.*

—Peter Drucker

L ike most childhoods, mine had its challenges. Yet I realize
now that I was fortunate in my upbringing in every sense
of the word. One of my earliest memories is traveling to live for
a year in New York City with my mother, who was getting her
master's degree in early childhood education. For a five-year-old
boy from North Carolina, learning to ice-skate on the rink at
Rockefeller Center was high adventure. The memory of eating
warm chestnuts bought from street vendors on cold afternoons
still brings a smile. Upon our return home, my father commented
that I sounded like a little Yankee. I never fully regained a southern accent. I consider my hybrid speech a memento of my unusual fortune in experiencing that happy time.

While both of my parents had achieved a great deal of success in their lives, I understood that their success was built on the economic and, in a sense, spiritual foundation laid by my grandparents. Both of my maternal grandparents were college graduates, a rarity for African Americans in the first half of the twentieth century. My grandmother, Rheba Hoffman, was a librarian and spoke fluent French. My grandfather, Guy, was a high school principal. As the owners of a Ford Model T and a house that they had built themselves on 41 acres of Tennessee property, they were solid citizens of a growing middle class. Rheba used her Singer sewing machine, a staple of small business opportunities discussed later in the chapter, to make and repair clothes. Together, my grandparents grew crops, raised an assortment of pigs and chickens, and hired help to manage their household and land. They considered themselves well-off by any standard. As African Americans in the South during the 1930s, they were exceptionally secure.

At that time, many people, especially black people, could rarely afford to fill their car's gas tank. Even if you could afford to buy a car, being able to afford to drive it was another matter. A favorite family story—retold by a friend who, as a teenager, had pumped gas in town—recounted a day when my grandfather pulled up to the gas station in his Model T. The young service attendant asked Principal Hoffman how much gas he wanted in the tank. My grandfather then inquired how much the tank would hold. When the reply was, "About 10 gallons," he promptly declared, "Well, fill it up, boy! Fill it up!" The story got many laughs, but we also got the message—my grandfather was a prosperous man.

Yet if the Hoffmans of the 1930s were to walk into a typical middle-class suburban home today, they might well feel something akin to awe. They might even believe they'd arrived in a small palace owned by people of fabulous means. The home's central heating and air-conditioning, washer and dryer, refrigerator, freezer, dishwasher, multiple TVs, computers, microwave ovens, and automatic sprinklers—not to mention several cars—would signal one thing: extreme financial wealth.

The contrast between my grandparents' good life and many Americans' lives today illustrates an interesting phenomenon—namely, that our definition of wealth is constantly changing. This is true not only in the United States, but in all cultures and countries of the world. The lifestyle and possessions that we take for granted today as almost the birthright of a twenty-first-century American would have been unthinkable even for a land baron of the nineteenth century. We can also predict with some certainty that the items that we consider luxuries today will be viewed as ordinary conveniences tomorrow. For example, when I was a young child in the 1950s, most families aspired to have a single TV in the living room. Today, it's not uncommon to find TVs in the living room, kitchen, family room, and most bedrooms in a single house. A "home theater," once the privilege of elite homeowners and Hollywood moguls, has now become almost commonplace in suburban America.

The fluidity of what wealth means to us—both as individuals and as a society—shows that wealth and our expectations of its rewards are in the eye of the beholder. The yardstick for measuring wealth keeps evolving. The manner in which European settlers in America accumulated and viewed wealth changed dramatically during the Industrial Revolution. When the Information Age arrived, the means and measurements of wealth evolved yet again. The common denominator, however, remains the same: a deep desire to make a better life.

The yardstick for measuring wealth keeps evolving.

The Era of Basic Necessities

I consider my grandparents to have been pioneers in a distinctly American tradition. Their determination to own land, depend on themselves, and create a prosperous life reflects the desires and courage that lie at the heart of an American ideal. It was these very desires that drove the earliest European immigrants to leave the comfort and certainty of their known world and come to a New World that was utterly unfamiliar and potentially hostile. My own ancestors first came to these shores for different reasons and under drastically different circumstances. Yet it was the profound universality of these dreams of self-determination that led my ancestors to work so hard to fulfill those dreams—once they had the opportunity to do so.

My ancestors' experiences, and the contrasts I can observe in the relatively brief time since my grandparents' coming of age, have piqued my curiosity. How and why have we as a society traveled so far and so quickly? Are there lessons about the psychology of wealth to be gleaned from that journey?

Many of the Europeans who crossed the ocean were seeking the opportunity to chart a new life course, free from the authority of the monarchies back home. Being able to farm land of their own, to hunt, to feed their families, and to worship as they chose represented a significant step up in the quality of their lives. The freedom they found is an example of a type of wealth that is timeless and priceless in all cultures.

Yet we know that for the first 150 years or so, life for these settlers and their descendants was difficult and sometimes even deadly. Many conveniences had been available to people in Europe, even those in the poorer segments of society. In this strange new land, simply meeting life's basic requirements was a daily challenge. Many people suddenly found themselves measuring their position in life on the most primal of scales: by their ability to secure food, shelter, and physical safety. The line between life and death sometimes depended on a turn in the weather and, as a result, a potential failure of the food supply. For this reason, the long period of America's early economic development—from around 1607 to 1790—may best be described as the "era of basic necessities." For most people, mastery of the land and its fruits were the benchmarks of individual success—and survival.

The Land of Opportunity = The Opportunity for Land

In the New World's developing agrarian economy, as in much of the Old World, land ownership offered the best opportunity for achieving a measure of prosperity. Most people relied on farming for their livelihood and for opportunities for financial growth. Some also traded with Native Americans or exported goods to Europe. But for the average individual, prosperity meant owning a home and growing enough food to feed one's family, and perhaps also having a few head of livestock. A horse and buggy to haul oneself and one's supplies into and out of town was a necessity as well. Having more than one horse and extra crops to sell equaled abundance.

America has long been considered a land of opportunity, and for good reason. While most new Americans sustained themselves in traditional ways, the source of greatest wealth was the ownership of large amounts of land. The vast amounts of undeveloped land in the Americas held nearly limitless opportunities for privileged families. The holders of the largest tracts, the gentry of the New World, had the benefit of being able to produce excess food and secure the services of indentured workers. This excess production enabled the first accumulation of financial wealth in the New World.

This New World gentry was made up of Europeans who had been given the rights to huge tracts of land in the colonies. The governments of England, the Netherlands, and Spain bought or took hundreds of thousands of acres from Native Americans and granted them to families and individuals with high status or influence in Europe. Charters were also granted to business ventures, such as the Massachusetts Bay Company, whose activities could benefit the mother country. The beneficiaries of these grants had full authority over the income created from their stewardship of the land (although they were also heavily taxed by the mother country), and their wealth grew exponentially. In some of the eastern colonies established by England, this arrangement gave these landed families and their heirs the rights to own, sell, inherit, or will their land, and to buy additional land from others.

The climate of the southern colonies was conducive to developing large farms and plantations. As the population of the American colonies grew, agriculture prevailed in the South, and commerce progressed more readily in the North. Relying on slave labor, southern planters expanded production and, with it, their fortunes. In the antebellum South, aristocratic lifestyles emerged. Wealth was blossoming in America for these flourishing landowners.

As settlements in the American colonies continued to grow and cities developed, a second wave of well-connected immigrants arrived. Initially settling in the Northeast, some of these privileged immigrants founded commercial and investment banks, trading companies, and other businesses that eventually produced tremendous riches. To preserve their power and influence, these new Americans formed partnerships and business alliances that kept their money and holdings within their immediate families, or at least within a close circle of friends. These financial giants would eventually help fund the American Revolution and, later, the Civil War. Their vast financial holdings exemplified extreme wealth and power in the first two centuries of New World growth.

In early America, there were wide economic gaps between large landholders and those who worked the land, but the desire for self-determination that had brought many of the first immigrants to this hemisphere was already having its influence. This desire was to drive America's economic future and spark the world-shaking political upheaval of the American Revolution. The fulfillment of this desire by many new Americans was laying the foundation for the unique philosophy that still underlies the nation's collective consciousness: life, liberty, and the pursuit of happiness.

From Land to Mass Production: The Industrial Revolution

With the Americans' victory in the Revolutionary War in 1783, the last remnants of the old political and economic influences of Europe gave way, and the first stages of a uniquely American era of wealth and prosperity began to take shape. In this new democracy, virtually anyone had the opportunity to create wealth.

This period was also the beginning of the Industrial Revolution, when the ways in which wealth was made and measured changed radically. Between 1790 and the 1830s, wealth began to take on a new identity in both the United States and Europe, as the world witnessed the triumph of a middle class of industrialists and businessmen. In America, as these men grew in affluence, they assumed positions of power and influence that previously had been limited to the landed class of nobility and aristocracy. Although only a relative few achieved this type of wealth, the growth of prosperity in America was tremendous.

The American Industrial Revolution began with the opening of the first industrial cotton mill in 1790. Samuel Slater built the mill in Rhode Island with machinery designed on a British model. Within 10 years, at least 50 other Slater-style mills were operating in the United States, greatly increasing textile production. An early form of outsourcing supported this expansion: small pieces of textile work were performed in people's homes. This new approach to organizing the workload was the forerunner of the factory system, in which workers performed large amounts of work in a single facility. Many of the workers in this new environment were women, who, in the process, gained more independence from the family farm.

In the United States, the transition from an agricultural and mercantile economy to an industrial one took more than a century. Industrial advancement in America lagged somewhat behind that in Great Britain because of the immense amount of land requiring development, coupled with a relative shortage of labor. However, with the advent of American innovations in transportation, manufacturing, and machinery, the U.S. economy steadily progressed and soon caught up, and a new age of productivity was born. With it came a much higher standard of living for many people.

The Era of Basic Conveniences

Yet another change would be needed, however, to support the growth of this new economy, and that change was in credit. More sources of credit—and, with it, capital—became necessary to help businesses develop. By 1805, the Bank of the United States, chartered by Congress in 1791 at Alexander Hamilton's urging, had opened offices in eight major cities and was financing fledgling businesses. After Congress failed to renew the federal bank's charter in 1811, state governments continued to establish banks; within five years, they had launched more than 200 state-chartered banks and had taken on the responsibility for funding the growth of business. This created a swift and necessary increase of credit for the economy. Unfortunately, not all the banks were properly regulated; this poor oversight created an economic crisis that led to a depression in 1819.[1] America went from galloping expansion to its first major economic depression, the likes of which wouldn't be experienced again until the Great Depression of the 1920s and 1930s. However, this crisis provided a valuable lesson: to benefit society, growth and debt must be managed wisely.

To benefit society, growth and debt must be managed wisely.

Fast Forward to 2008

As most of us are keenly aware, in 2008, failures of major banks and insurance companies sparked an economic crisis that brought credit markets to a grinding halt. A series of collapses in the mortgage industry also contributed to the financial ruin of millions. The effects of these failures and the crisis in confidence rippled through much of the world, causing even more economic damage and hardship.[2] Had we not learned the lessons of earlier hard times?

A Story of Personal Circumstances

The pastoral setting of Bill and Deb Mann's home, on the banks of the Cumberland River in Tennessee, might lead you to believe that you had stepped back in time. Set on a hill, the house, with a big screened porch, overlooks the river and a garden with irises and butterfly bushes. "It's so peaceful here," Deb says. "It is like breathing in the nectar of God."

But like many others in the United States, Bill and Deb's house is being repossessed. Even with Deb's nine years of experience in real estate development, they weren't able to get ahead of the crash. It's been tough, but Deb and Bill feel that they have learned a lot. They believe theirs is a story of personal circumstances, some of which were extraordinary and some of which were shared by many other people. Bill explained, "When the economic collapse occurred, we lost all of our real estate investments. Then a 500-year flood hit our hometown. It damaged our home and completely took out my mom's house. Then my mom became ill."

This isn't the way they would like to have written their story, but they are learning to get their finances in order, and they know they'll get through it. They have started a small business, and Bill continues to work as a musician. He concludes, "It's about perseverance. It has been stressful, but there are still blessings. People in the community have helped rebuild my mother's house, and we'll all be moving in there soon." He's optimistic about the future. Despite our society's collective amnesia about previous hard times, history tells us that he's right to feel that way.

So what caused the economic near-meltdown that was felt from Wall Street to the Cumberland River and to many other hillsides and streets in the United States? Nobel laureate Paul Krugman believes that "Regulation didn't keep up with the system."[3] In the balancing act of uninhibited expansion and judicious oversight, we have clearly been dropping a few balls. To figure out how we might pick them up again and, in the process, create better personal relationships with money, a closer look at credit is needed.

Prosperity for All

Historically, the ability to borrow money has often been a privilege that was restricted to the wealthy. Borrowing allowed people who already had money to borrow more in order to make investments, which often made them wealthier. For the growth of the American economy, it was important that many more people should have access to such mainstream credit. The opening of bank credit to middle-class business owners played a key role in the expansion of American prosperity. Without credit, whole groups of people would have remained locked in a type of caste system from which it was difficult, if not impossible, to escape.

As the doors to lending and borrowing opportunities opened wider, middle-class Americans were better able to start and support businesses, resulting in greater prosperity for all. This also marked the beginning of a more modern view of borrowing and lending. These activities lost their stigma when money was lent to business owners who used it to move ahead in life. "Credit is the vital air of the system of modern commerce," Daniel Webster wrote in 1834. "It has done more, a thousand times, to enrich nations than all the mines of all the world."

This kind of financing proceeded briskly at all levels of the industrial economy. Yet new forms of credit were needed to enable the further expansion of American prosperity. Between 1840 and 1890, these changes began to take place with the expansion of consumer lending. Before that time, borrowing for reasons other than investment was frowned upon. Obtaining credit to buy items for individual consumption was considered an indulgence—something done merely to satisfy personal desire. This kind of borrowing was called "consumptive credit." In contrast, loans to purchase such items as farm machinery could be justified as "productive credit"—that is, purchases that would contribute to income rather than depreciate over time.

But in 1856, the perception and function of consumer borrowing began to change. A revolution in the way Americans live had begun—with the humble sewing machine. The Singer Sewing Machine Company introduced its retail installment credit plan. The program was clear and catchy: "a dollar down, a dollar a week" to buy a sewing machine on credit and repay the loan. Right away, this credit plan allowed a great many more families to purchase sewing machines.

This simple program was a powerful spur to the advancement of the middle class and the further rise of prosperity in America. Many women's diaries from that period portray sewing by hand as one of the most time-consuming of domestic tasks. The Singer machine dramatically reduced the time required for this activity. For example, the time needed to make a shirt dropped from fourteen hours to just one. This new efficiency allowed enterprising housewives to take on activities that earned money—up to a dollar a day. Since the sewing machine cost a dollar a week, the debt was highly productive and greatly enhanced the women's prosperity. Some women made names for themselves through their refined and original efforts, and the machines provided many women with a type of freedom they hadn't known before.

A Peach in South Carolina

Margaret Campbell Bailey was born in Ruby, South Carolina, in 1925. She is called Peachie, both for the peach grove in which she grew up and for the healthy pink color of her cheeks. Peachie reminisces, "It was hard times back then, but my mother was smart. She never let us know we were poor." Peachie's mother was also enterprising. While staying at home with her children, she earned extra money by sewing clothing for other people. Peachie says, "To make a dress, she got 25 cents. My mother made everything we wore from top to bottom. The only thing I don't think Mama made was Daddy's Sunday clothes. But she did make the white suit my sister got married in. She sewed it from the bags that held the soda we bought for the crops. When washed and starched, that cloth was like fine linen. It was beautiful.

"That sewing machine was in the house from the time I can remember. They bought it with installment payments, because no one had enough money to buy a sewing machine outright back then."

One Easter, nine-year-old Peachie didn't have an Easter dress. "My mother had surgery, and afterward they wouldn't let her pedal a machine for a while. I cried because this meant I wouldn't have an Easter dress. Mama told me that if I would do the pedaling, she would help me. She showed me how to lay out her homemade pattern, and I cut the pieces out of washed and pressed feedsack cloth. Mama sat beside me and put the pieces together. Then she would say, 'Now sew that.' I made my dress, and I have been sewing ever since."

When Sacony Sewing Company opened mills in South Carolina, Peachie went to work for them. "Later, when I went back to working for myself, I sewed for three ladies who worked at Prudential, Western Electric, and Gifford Mills. Ladies were coming up in the workplace and needed dresses for work. I charged 10 dollars per dress and could make four to five dresses per day. It was hard work, with 10- to 12-hour days, but I was making pretty good money. I've done pretty well for myself."

And the Singer Sewing Machine Company? It did more than any other business or institution to bring the installment plan to the world. In the process, the company grew to be among the first multinational corporations.

Prospecting for Prosperity

Anne Norton's great-great-grandfather was the first salesman of Singer sewing machines in Louisville, Kentucky. Anne still has the first sewing machine the family bought when he worked for Singer. Its walnut case and heavy cast-iron work are things of beauty. After the Civil War, women who had lost their husbands during the war headed west to seek better prospects. In the American West in the late nineteenth century, there was little ready-made clothing. Women saw their sewing machines as passports to greater prosperity. Their machines provided them not only with financial security, but with more value for prospective husbands. For many women, a Singer sewing machine had become the most prized of possessions. Among other benefits to western women, the machines, along with mail-order patterns and fabrics, assured them that they could be as fashionable as their sisters in the eastern cities they had left behind.[4]

In the last few decades of the nineteenth century, installment credit programs similar to Singer's were rapidly adopted to sell other useful household items.[5] With these loan programs, the window of opportunity opened for average citizens to make purchases and upgrade their living standards in ways that had previously been out of reach.[6] Ownership of certain durable goods—sewing machines, fine furniture, and large machinery to work a farm— was regarded as a means to progress in life in material ways.[7]

I was also surprised to learn about the piano's role in this progress to prosperity. Historically, owning a piano had been a privilege restricted to royalty. Even as piano prices came down, they were not affordable for anyone but the aristocracy. Installment credit plans changed that. And when pianos became accessible to ordinary wage earners, the instrument's popularity soared. Having a piano provided a sense of gentility in a frontier environment. Everywhere in America, piano ownership represented solid citizenship in the middle class.

Sammy Kicklighter, of Brevard, North Carolina,[8] is a purveyor of pianos and an amateur historian of the instrument. He explained that in the late 1800s, "a piano offered both refinement and at-home entertainment when there was little such diversion otherwise. If you could afford a piano, the implication was that you were in the company of kings. It gave prestige to the family. With the introduction of player pianos and smaller uprights, the country saw a virtual piano boom." In 1850, fewer than 50,000 pianos were manufactured worldwide. Between 1890 and 1928, U.S. sales of pianos ranged from 172,000 to 364,000 per year.[9] Installment credit plans brought pianos to Americans, and more Americans to the installment plan.[10]

Henry Ford Changes the World

Enter the automobile. Henry Ford didn't invent cars, but he brought them within the economic reach of large numbers of people. In the process, he changed just about everything in American life. Charles Sorensen joined Henry Ford as an executive at Ford Motor Company while Ford was designing the Model T. Sorensen described how he was brought to a secret room at the company. "Early one morning in the winter of 1906–07, Henry Ford dropped in at the pattern department of the Piquette Avenue plant to see me. 'Come with me, Charlie,' he said, 'I want to show you something.' I followed him to the third floor and . . . he looked about and said, 'Charlie, I'd like to have a room finished off right here in this space.'" Ford described his requirements for the utmost secrecy for the room that would hold the blueprints and patents for the car. Sorensen said, "It became the maternity ward for Model T."[11]

Although Ford did everything he could to keep the Model T affordable, it still cost almost a year's salary for most people. And so a new arena of commerce was born—third-party automobile finance companies. By 1925, as much as 75 percent of cars were being purchased on an installment plan. Credit financing was again shortening the road to upward mobility for the middle class.

With the Industrial Revolution, the yardstick for measuring prosperity in the average home had again changed. In addition to owning middle-class status symbols, such as a piano, a family's ability to pay others to produce their food and their basic necessities—and the leisure time provided by machines of all kinds—signified that the family had earned its piece of the American dream. By the twentieth century, the United States had completed its geographical expansion into the immense western lands and was looking to a future that promised endless economic development. During this time, the United States also began to take on a leadership role in world trade and industry.

With the rapid escalation of the Information Age, prosperity now looks unlike any of its previous incarnations.

Wealth in the Information Age—The Era of Basic Luxuries

In the last few decades, our measuring stick for wealth in America has stretched yet again—and almost as dramatically as it did during the Industrial Revolution. With the rapid escalation of the Information Age, prosperity now looks unlike any of its previous incarnations. Indeed, the lifestyle that a contemporary American might consider merely comfortable surpasses what a colonial family would have deemed fabulous wealth. In many ways, the twenty-first-century Joneses' minimum requirements would be unimaginable even to John Jacob Astor, considered to be the richest man in America when he died in 1848. Perhaps even more striking is the fact that many aspects of our lifestyle today would seem like a fantasy to the American Joneses of even several decades ago.

Much of this shift is due to the explosion of technology over the last 30 years. Today, virtually no one in America or in many other parts of the world lives without a cell phone, a device that was seen only in science fiction not long ago. Powerful and portable personal computers, including smartphones, are nearly ubiquitous. These devices, along with high-speed Internet access and the almost limitless power it gives individuals to connect, create, learn, and earn, have revolutionized the way we live—and our expectations for wealth.

Today, for most "middle-class" citizens of the world, home-ownership is a mark of prosperity. Although the United States is experiencing a mortgage crisis, it remains a prosperous nation. According to the U.S. Department of Commerce, 67 percent of Americans own the home in which they live. The National Association of Home Builders found that the average home size in the United States had expanded to 2,700 square feet in 2009, which was 1,400 square feet more than the size of an average home in 1970. Most middle-class Americans, *Time* reported, not only hold a mortgage but have a "professional or managerial job that earns them somewhere between $30,000 and $100,000 a year."[12] In addition, 70 percent also "have cable and two or more cars. Two-thirds have high-speed Internet, and forty percent own a flat-screen TV. They have several credit cards each and a lot of luxury goods." Yet tellingly, most members of America's middle class "still believe that others have more than they do."[13] For most people, prosperity includes not only the assets described above, but also the ability to travel by air for business and leisure, a modest savings account, a retirement plan, and life and health insurance. Friends and good health round out the picture of what most Americans consider a satisfactory degree of happiness and material comfort. Affluence only *begins* with these fundamentals and might also include a vacation home, private schooling for their kids, exotic travel, ever-renewed wardrobe and jewelry, a generous retirement plan, lucrative investments, and so on.

Today, what we now consider basic necessities—such as washers, dryers, vacuum cleaners, and cars—are within the reach of most Americans, even many of those whom the U.S. Census Bureau classifies as "poor." The widespread ownership of these items showcases a welcome rise in our overall standard of living. And yet it raises a question: has the perpetual stretching of the yardstick for prosperity distorted our expectation of what a satisfactory lifestyle should include?

In part, this stretch reflects our innate human desire to grow and reach beyond ourselves—and in several ways we are growing and evolving at an unprecedented rate. As this growth occurs, the challenge is to become more conscious of our own hopes, dreams, and actions. This means, in part, not being swept up by the cultural drive to own and spend more—specifically, more than we can handle while maintaining a balanced and prosperous life.

Some of this growth in the yardstick for wealth is certainly caused by a bombardment of media messages that are not necessarily in our best interest. We are assailed daily with advertisements for newer, better, and sexier cars, gadgets, and conveniences. We are exhorted to vacation in faraway places, dine out every night, and generally accumulate more and more. We are told how we should feel, smell, eat, drink, look, and play. If we don't feel as fabulous—or live as well—as the radiantly smiling people on TV, we're told what drug we can take to make ourselves feel better. While advertising is an essential engine of the economy of most developed nations, its messages can act as distractions.

Yet we have taken the bait. Many people have been accumulating possessions at an alarming rate, using credit to build a house of cards. Debt is massive and climbing, and it threatens to wreak havoc on our individual and collective lives. Has credit, one of the developments that helped create wealth in America and other parts of the world, somehow become a bad thing? As I researched and learned more about what is happening to global and individual prosperity today, and where we've come from, answering this question became more critical in my mind. It is clear that credit is as vital for prosperity and for national and individual growth as it has ever been. Without it, our economy would come to a crashing halt. So what's the answer? I needed to learn more.

In the meantime, it was not difficult to see that people need more from life than lots of possessions and lots of money. According to a 2010 analysis, the three wealthiest cities in the world are New York, London, and Paris. This analysis was based on four indexes that measure economic vitality, political influence, research ability, and standard of living. Yet, surprisingly, the countries with the happiest citizens don't include any of these cities. The Better Life Index, created by the Organization for Economic Cooperation and Development (OECD), measures countries by categories that include housing, income, community, education, environment, governance, health, life satisfaction, and other factors. Based on these categories, Australia and Canada are tied for having the happiest residents. The next four countries, in order, are New Zealand, Denmark, Norway, and Sweden.[14]

In 2009, the Gallup-Healthways Well-Being Index showed that New York, the wealthiest city in the world, was not even among the top 10 happiest U.S. cities. The happiest was Boulder, Colorado, an economically modest burg in comparison.[15] The good life is clearly about far more than having and spending. True prosperity and happiness are obviously tied to the intangibles of life.

The Next Evolution

From the twists and turns of history, I had learned that wealth is a fluid concept. Our view of the good life has changed and evolved around the world, which is good news for us as individuals. If the definition of wealth is changeable, it implies that we have the opportunity to discover and define what wealth means to us personally—and to take steps to achieve it.

We want more from life—and the things we want cannot be put on our credit cards. Commercials tell us that certain aspects of life are priceless, but what does that really mean? Ultimately, it is up to us as individuals to find the meaning of prosperity, and that takes conscious consideration. If there's something more to happiness and prosperity than financial assets, each of us must consider the question: what is my personal yardstick for wealth, and how did I come by it? We will attempt to solve these puzzles on our way to discovering how to find and fulfill our own dreams of prosperity.

Finding Your Dream

*If we all did the things we are capable
of doing, we would literally astound
ourselves.*

—Thomas Alva Edison

My family history in America began with slavery. Few beginnings of any life are as crushing to a sense of self or as difficult to overcome. Yet from these hard beginnings came my inheritance of family treasure—stories of courage, perseverance, hard work, and almost unimaginable fortitude.

My great-great-grandparents James and Hattie Riles were born into slavery and as young adults were set free by the Emancipation Proclamation. These new citizens of South Carolina then walked to Greenville, Tennessee. There they managed to purchase 41 acres of property—the same acres that my grandparents Guy and Rheba owned two generations later. James was fair-skinned and was able to buy his land, in part, by "passing" for white. Both he and Hattie had been fathered by white plantation owners whose identities have been lost to history. Not lost is the story that Hattie had been ordered to work as a house slave, but, to avoid her mother's fate, had asked for and gained the much harder job of working in the fields. In Tennessee, my newly freed great-great-grandparents grew fruits and vegetables. The word is that James had a green thumb and could grow anything, including ginseng. Hattie was the keeper of the purse, and a strict one.

Today my great-great-grandparents' land, that sweet piece of Tennessee, remains a family heritage. Yet even more precious to me are the values that my family has lived by and taught to each succeeding generation. From my family, I've learned that an invisible balance sheet is passed to us from those who came before. Becoming aware of and understanding my family's balance sheet and the hard-won entries on it has helped me immeasurably in becoming who I am today. The pride I feel in my ancestors, and the lessons I have learned, have guided me every step of the way. I have absorbed, both consciously and unconsciously, some of the habits, values, and strengths that earlier generations called upon to build their own interesting lives. Through them—and through my own trials and errors of self-discovery—I've managed to create a life that I treasure.

Net Worth and Self-Worth

There are plenty of books that profess to tell you how to achieve financial riches. I am neither an accountant nor an economist. As a psychotherapist, my expertise is in helping people to become more self-aware, find perspective, and take meaningful steps toward achieving their full potential. Part of this process of self-discovery is picking apart the messages that they have internalized about themselves that may or may not be true—and then finding what is indeed true for each person.

Just as each part of a hologram contains the essence of the entire image, each unique element of an individual psyche—such as self-worth, a sense of humor, interests, biases, passions, and general outlook on life—reflects and affects the whole and contributes to the person's overall life experience. All of our attitudes and beliefs are in some way manifested in each individual part of our lives. Because of this correlation, our relationship with money mirrors the quality of the other relationships in our lives and our ability to achieve true prosperity.

Each of us carries conscious and unconscious beliefs about ourselves—and about what we can expect to achieve—from childhood into adulthood. I believe that to effect a positive change in your relationship with money, it is important that you have a clear picture of who you are, where you came from, and where you want to go. It is only when you know what prosperity means to you personally that you can start to move toward it. When you know this, you can begin to make conscious choices that lead to your financial goals—and any other objectives that your dreams, creativity, and motivation dictate.

The road to happiness lies in two simple principles: find what interests you and you can do well, and put your whole soul into it—every bit of energy and ambition and natural ability you have. —John D. Rockefeller

As a self-employed individual, my personal income has surpassed that of both my parents combined. By their standards, I've achieved a degree of personal wealth. But am I wealthy? From a certain financial perspective, perhaps not. Today it would take at least $7.6 million to have the purchasing power of $1 million in 1959. While I am financially comfortable, my financial assets currently fall far short of that mark. However, my sense of internal wealth and personal fulfillment is at an all-time high. I thoroughly enjoy my life. Step by step, I have built a life in which

I find meaning in my work, can pursue projects that excite me, and can share the adventure of it with people I love.

For many of us, our relationship with money—and the amount that we have or don't have—is what most readily defines our sense of wealth and prosperity. This is true not just because the financial balance sheet is our society's most easily recognized measure of success and failure, but also because wealth seems intrinsically connected to the accumulation of assets. Yet people still sense that true prosperity encompasses more than money and that, at times, being as rich as a king can lead to a "poverty of riches."

To achieve a prosperous life requires a clear understanding of our own values, and keeping our vision of that life clearly in front of us. To create a life that is rich in what matters to us (whether or not that includes an abundance of money), we must, in fact, understand what we want. And we must understand how our expectations and our self-image prepare us for success or for something less. Doing so requires us to look at our culture, our personal past, and the future we envision for ourselves.

Where exactly do our values concerning money, achievement, and self-worth come from? While we are growing up, we naturally internalize the lessons and values of our environment, including those of our family and of the larger society in which we live. Because we are social animals, our society's collective attitudes play a disproportionate role in our psyche. Understanding this influence is essential. The psychology of wealth is a delicate weave of social and family yardsticks and our own sense of what "worth" and prosperity mean. Bringing all these threads to consciousness is the first step in achieving our vision of a prosperous life.

Stories of our family's heritage may enhance our self-esteem or diminish it. The lessons that society and our family instilled in us as children can sometimes run counter to our personal vision of prosperity—the qualities that we value as individuals. When that's the case, it takes a healthy sense of self-worth to achieve one's vision and maintain it. To have a feeling of abundance, we must feel worthy of having it.

Society tells us that being wealthy means having a heap of money and material assets. It is certainly easy to calculate our net worth in these terms. For example, Thomas J. Stanley and William D. Danko, authors of the book *The Millionaire Next Door: The Surprising Secrets of America's Wealthy*, offer a simple formula.[1] They propose that you multiply your age by your total pretax household income, add the amount of any inheritances, and then divide that number by 10. The resulting figure is your net worth. However, if we accept that definition of net worth— or any definition of wealth that doesn't include the intangibles of life—we might overlook the very things that make life precious and fulfilling.

The Role of Family and Family Culture

Perhaps an even more powerful influence on our values and our sense of worth than that of society is the family culture in which we were raised—in other words, our family operating system. Did you emerge from your family operating system with a sense of acceptance and worth simply for being who you are? Or was your value tied primarily to your external accomplishments and gains? Family culture, in turn, is influenced by the greater culture in which a family forms. With the publication of the book *Battle Hymn of the Tiger Mother*, by Amy Chua,[2] the debate was on: which cultures produce adults with the highest levels of success and self-esteem? Let's consider two: the Asian-style and the American-style family operating systems.

As Chua captures in her book, the stereotypical Asian parents link self-worth to a high level of personal achievement and recognition by others. They define clearly what they want their children to achieve, then drive them toward those goals through discipline, self-sacrifice, and delayed gratification. In this family operating system, a powerful external pressure for excellence rules a child's upbringing. Consequently, any failure to reach the parents' predetermined goals can erode a child's sense of worthiness and success. The lines separating love, achievement, self-worth, ambition, and pride are blurred.

This emphasis on achievement can make children feel that parental love is dependent solely on what the child accomplishes. Unfortunately, kids who are raised with this message can turn into anxiety-ridden adults who never feel good enough. I've met outwardly successful people who have grown up this way and who feel stuck in a career that's not personally fulfilling. Sadly, there are many professionals in every field who have worked hard to get to the top, only to discover that they never really wanted what they have achieved and don't know what to do next. An internal feeling of wealth, success, and happiness never seems to materialize. These hardworking men and women never quite feel that they've "made it." They continue on their life path through a sense of obligation. The true worth of their own desires and a sense of what real prosperity would look like elude them.

In contrast to the stereotypical Asian model is the common perception of the American-style family operating system. In this stereotype, American moms and dads are far more indulgent than their Asian counterparts. American bookstores abound with parenting guides exhorting us to boost our children's self-esteem by giving them lavish praise and frequent assurances of their "specialness." Although we as Americans value winners, awards and ribbons are given to every child, sometimes simply for showing up to a contest. In short—and perhaps admirably—stereotypical American children are loved and accepted simply for being who they are.

In this stereotype, however, parents place few demands on their children and have few specific expectations for them. They are unsystematic about helping children to define their goals and teaching them to plan paths to financial independence and prosperity. For example, Americans place a high value on education, yet many people pursue a university degree without a clear intention of how they plan to use it. As a result, an American child often feels loved and cared for, but, as an adult, can have mixed success in the areas of impulse control and goal setting. In this stereotype, children grow up to be self-indulgent underachievers.

Both of these stereotypical styles of parenting have their pitfalls, yet both have something valuable to teach us. The tremendous advantage of the traditional Asian family operating system is that goals, both small and large, and the steps to achieve them are defined explicitly. The value of self-discipline, work, and accomplishment in creating a prosperous life is ingrained early and often. Any individual who applies these principles has a distinct advantage in achieving a specific goal, financial or otherwise. The advantage of American-style parenting is that it leaves no question in the child's heart that she is valued and loved. And with Americans' inclination toward inspiration, creativity, and enthusiasm, these children are often much freer to define what happiness means to them as individuals and to follow their own hearts.

Most fortunate are those children who have parents that both love them unconditionally *and* make a healthy level of demands, while expressing realistic expectations for responsibility and achievement. This is a winning formula for growing into adulthood with a thriving sense of self-worth and well-ingrained habits of goal setting and accomplishment.

Although it is the rare individual who scales the summit of true greatness in any field, taking the steps toward our own goals calls upon what is greatest in ourselves.

Breaking Through the Bars

Financial educator Rickie Keys, whom I introduced in the first chapter, met me one weekend to talk over dinner. He's a confident and successful man, and I am always impressed with his openness. As mentioned, Rickie grew up in perhaps the worst inner-city neighborhood in the United States. He had no father in the home, and his mother worked three jobs. Yet today his life is exceptionally happy and full. He credits his mom and her relentless combination of toughness and love for his ability to have moved from such rough circumstances to where he is today.

"It seemed almost impossible that we could get out of our situation," he begins, "but it was not impossible to my mother. And that made all the difference. She *assumed* we would go to college and be successful. She took our training seriously, and she was tough. I credit her for instilling in my brother and me a sense of self-esteem and self-respect. She taught us aggressively, and she was hard on us. Even at the time, I knew she was hard on us. But we learned what we should and, most definitely, what we should not do. She taught us right from wrong. We weren't resentful, but we did not like it. Sure, we were sort of sad at times; we thought it would have been more fun to play in the streets with the other kids. We had bars on our windows that you could not break through—heavy bars. My brother and I would do our homework and look down at the street where the other boys were playing ball. And the kids would sing, 'Ha, ha, ha, Rickie and Jeffrey are in jail!' Now, sadly, many of those kids are either really in jail or dead. My brother and I both made it out. We're grateful now for our mom's toughness—very grateful.

"We received positive affirmations from her, definitely. That is part of good parenting, and my mom took it seriously," Rickie says. "When we did something right, she would honor, praise, and acknowledge us—everything a good parent should do. She said, 'You can do it.' But she was 'old school.' She'd say, 'You can do anything—and if you don't do what you're supposed to do' . . . well, there were consequences. But for that reason, when she told us we could be successful, we believed her. Without a single, solitary doubt, we believed her. Despite the appalling environment, despite the poverty all around us and the negative influences everywhere, hers was the voice that pulled us through."

Rickie feels blessed with his mother's love and her determination to impress on her boys that education was required if they were going to rise out of the neighborhood. He says, "My mom believed in being responsible. And she did her best. She also believed that you need to take care of the next generation. When she passed away, remarkably, she left enough insurance money to take care of my children's education."

If your family's operating system didn't encompass both, or either, of these values—discipline and unconditional love—you may have started out in life with a disadvantage. You may have a less than sturdy sense of self-esteem and some doubts about your ability to achieve what you want in life. If this is true, your climb to prosperity and self-worth may be somewhat steeper. However, that doesn't mean that you can't achieve everything you set your heart and mind on.

Although it is the rare individual who scales the summit of true greatness in any field, taking the steps toward our own goals calls upon what is greatest in ourselves. And greatness comes in many guises.

Every Step Up

If you didn't grow up with a healthy family operating system and a good standing within it, or if the system you grew up in didn't encourage a healthy self-image and self-disciplined habits, how do you grow beyond such limitations and develop those things for yourself?

Studies show that there is a strong link between self-worth and a sense of achievement. To build self-esteem, human beings must face and meet challenges. It isn't enough for your parents or others to simply tell you that you're good, strong, or smart. You must experience your own ability to accomplish something difficult or creative. You must experience firsthand your own competence and your ability to make something happen, to move things ahead. In other words, you must show *yourself* what you can do. By setting goals for yourself and achieving them, by being willing to take some failure on the chin and keep going—by taking some intelligent risks—you can build a sense of self-worth. This confidence won't be dependent on external validation or past experiences within your family.

And what if you didn't receive unconditional love from your caregivers as a child? This may be the saddest legacy of a less than ideal upbringing. Here again, though, it is never too late. You can cultivate the generosity and love in yourself that was missing from your childhood to create rich, supportive relationships in your life.

The Archetype of Wealth

Another way to uncover and strengthen your individual psychology of wealth is to look at wealth through the lens of a psychological archetype. In Jungian psychology, an archetype is defined as "a collectively inherited unconscious idea, pattern, thought, or image that is universally present in individual psyches." In other words, archetypes are concepts that we inherit simply by being human and that affect us unconsciously. Wealth is such an archetype. Examining the universal archetype of wealth can help us to understand the nature of wealth—and, most important, to begin discovering what it means to us as individuals.

Like everything in our universe, archetypes have a dual nature: right and left, up and down, light and dark, and hot and cold—each has two faces. One is the archetype's constructive, idealized expression; the other is its destructive, or shadow, expression. The archetype's constructive expression represents its highest potential for supporting positive growth and fulfillment. The shadow expression is the negative underside of the idea or pattern. The archetype of wealth has both these sides.

In order to develop a healthy psychology of wealth, we must recognize and come to terms with its archetype. When we recognize the nature of wealth—with its potential for supporting happiness and, conversely, with its pitfalls—we can use it to our advantage rather than allow it to unconsciously drive or sabotage us. Our individual concept of wealth can inspire and motivate us, or it can lead to stress and burnout. In its most extreme shadow expression, the underside of wealth can result in a chaotic life, prone to negativity, self-destructive behavior, and tragedy. To generate the life we want, we must reinforce the positive aspects of the wealth archetype in our awareness and actions.

THE NEGATIVE SIDE OF WEALTH IS

- Restrictive
- Miserly
- Self-serving
- Judgmental

The Negative Side of Wealth

The shadow, or destructive, side of the wealth archetype is restrictive, constrictive, suspicious, miserly, competitive, abusive, arrogant, self-serving, punitive, judgmental, indulgent, and disempowering. This side of wealth is driven by fear and insecurity. It is also accompanied by stress and anxiety, and often by lashing out and blaming others. Operating in this state floods the body with stress hormones and can actually lead to cardiovascular disease and other disorders of the heart.

I've coached talented executives and entrepreneurs who are good people, but who, each time they take on a new project, fear that they will be discovered to be frauds. They fear that they will be exposed as being inadequate to carry out the tasks at hand, regardless of their education or experience. Each day they soldier on, hoping that others keep believing that they're good enough, while not really believing it themselves. They have all the ingredients for wealth and prosperity, but they are missing the key element of self-confidence. As a result, they live with a perpetual, internal sense of lack and desperation.

Someone who is in the thrall of the shadow expression of wealth, no matter how much financial wealth has been accumulated, feels that resources are limited and therefore must be aggressively guarded and jealously protected. Driven by greed and fear, this person seeks ever greater accumulations of assets. The internal, negative viewpoint is that because resources are limited, the imperative is reduced to "I must get and protect mine before others do."

THE POSITIVE SIDE OF WEALTH IS

- Generous

- Proficient

- Creative

- Discerning

The Positive Side of Wealth

The positive expression of the wealth archetype encompasses four primary qualities: generosity, proficiency, creativity, and discernment. Thus, the idealized expression of the wealth archetype is generous, empowering, expansive, joyful, humorous, playful, enthusiastic, creative, regenerative, innovative, and service-oriented. At its core, this expression of wealth is never self-serving. Through the individual, it serves a higher cause or principle beyond the mere accumulation of assets. This principle may be spiritual, philanthropic, healing, patriotic, or otherwise positive and generous. Wealth becomes a vehicle to realize a more expansive goal of service in the world.

The creative expression of the wealth archetype recognizes that the world offers a nearly infinite abundance of resources, with more than enough to enrich those who have the desire and will to pursue their dreams. The person who embodies this face of the archetype has a constructive and expansive vision of wealth and develops it to encompass broader goals. The person who embraces this expression is dynamic and continually growing and evolving. Such individuals see not only their own potential, but that of others. They are positive and optimistic for themselves and encouraging of the people around them.

If your view of wealth includes these qualities, you will naturally attract like-minded people. Your inner sense of expansiveness and your willingness to grow will create situations in which you can experience the freedom to be your best. This may take hard work, perseverance, and everything you ever thought you had to give. With this generosity of spirit, however, you can begin from wherever you are to take your first steps toward wealth.

Moving Forward Consciously

How many times have you heard people lament that they've wound up in a life that they didn't anticipate and that doesn't fulfill their dreams? If you don't know where you want to go—if you are unconscious of what you want—ending up "somewhere else" may be the inevitable result. This result has certainly led many clients to my office. As you uncover the values you've internalized about wealth, however, you'll be in a much better position to make conscious choices about what wealth really means to you. You'll be better able to form your vision of a prosperous life. By becoming conscious of your true desires, you can start to make decisions that serve you rather than drive you. You will be able to act, rather than to be acted upon.

Darren Hardy, publisher and editorial director of *SUCCESS* magazine, is an expert on what makes an individual succeed. He works with people who exemplify the highest levels of achievement in all areas of their lives. Darren says, "The first step toward achieving your dreams and ambitions is to identify them. When you know exactly where you are going and focus on that endpoint, you will more directly and expeditiously reach your desired destination."[3]

FINDING YOUR CORE VALUES

What are your core values? A core value test will help you determine what is most important to you. Here's one to try: visit NetPlaces.com and search for "Core Values Test."

One way to identify your dreams and ambitions is to ask yourself: "What is my image of a prosperous life? How do I want to design my prototype of wealth and prosperity?" For you, is it performing meaningful work? Having the ability to travel? Having a loving and supportive mate with whom to share the road? Having a house in the country with kids in the yard? Finding the time to train for a marathon? Building a company that employs hundreds of your neighbors?

You can feel free to discard your hand-me-down beliefs about success, money, and wealth and upgrade them to fit values of your own choosing. To avoid selling yourself short, it is important that you periodically try stretching your goals a little bit. In your imagination, try stepping into a bigger room—a much bigger room. As Donald Trump famously says, "As long as you're going to be thinking anyway, think big."[4]

How do you follow this golden advice while making sure that you arrive at a place that pleases you? It takes some soul-searching, honesty, and a willingness to find what makes your heart sing. "Give yourself a little freedom to develop into something or someone you'd actually like to be,"[5] is another piece of sage advice from Donald Trump. In his book *Think Like a Champion: An Informal Education in Business and Life*,[6] this immensely successful businessman offers a remarkably spiritual suggestion for finding one's inner compass. In a section called "Give Your Higher Self a Chance," he writes: "Our higher self will often lead us into new waters, and for a good reason. No one wants to spend their life treading water just to keep from going under. That is futile and disheartening. Sometimes we do things to build up experience and stamina to prepare us, but it's to prepare us for something bigger. Always know you could be on the precipice of something great—that's being connected to your higher self. It's also a good way to keep those negative thoughts far away."

Armed with an awareness of what both success and prosperity mean to you, you can start to plan the steps that will lead you to your goals.

Working Without a Net

My longtime friend Marcus had the great fortune to be born into an affluent family with parents who loved him not only for his accomplishments, but simply for being their son. His father was a successful entrepreneur who trained Marcus from an early age to understand the family business and the importance of continuous learning. His father dearly wished that when Marcus grew up, he would take over the family enterprise, but as Marcus was reaching maturity, a different vision was taking root inside him— he had other dreams.

When Marcus was in his early twenties, he made a momentous decision: he would move away from his family's East Coast home and start a new life in California to pursue his own goal. There were no hard feelings; Marcus's father still respected and loved his son. But his dad made it clear that the law of cause and effect meant that if he walked away from the family business, he could not expect to inherit ownership in the company. Marcus agreed with the good sense in this and was happy for his brother, who would now inherit 100 percent of the business.

In California, Marcus's salary as the general manager of a small nonprofit organization barely covered his basic living expenses. He wasn't bothered by this. For Marcus, working for the nonprofit wasn't about money; rather, it was about devoting himself to a purpose he was passionate about. Because his work was meaningful to him, and he could see the positive fruits of his efforts every day, he was happy.

After many satisfying years of service with the nonprofit organization, Marcus had gained extensive international business experience. For his next adventure, he moved on to build a consulting firm that specialized in growing businesses. One of his clients was in the emerging organic foods industry. Marcus believed that the industry was on the cusp of explosive growth and was personally a longtime consumer of natural and organic foods. So he approached the founder and owner and offered to buy half the company. Upon the owner's acceptance of his offer, Marcus set to work expanding the company. Within a few years, he had turned it into the most successful natural foods company of its type in the United States. He later sold the company to an investment group for millions of dollars, while continuing to manage it as CEO for several years afterward.

In following his dream, Marcus had walked away from the safety net provided by his family and risked his financial advantages and security. He carried within his own psyche the seeds of wealth—courage, intelligence, a conscious and personalized vision of prosperity, and a sense of his own worth. By listening to his inner voice, he has created a life with meaning, purpose, and the personal freedom he had always envisioned.

A Shiny Black Limousine

Tony Cupisz's beginnings are perhaps the polar opposite of Marcus's. Yet today Tony and Marcus are both multimillionaires. As discussed in the first chapter, unlike Marcus, Tony did not come from a privileged background or even a stable home. His insight and understanding about how he emerged from that background are remarkable. His humility is striking. He wanted success, and despite all the reasons he could have used to give up on his dream and himself, he didn't.

When he entered college, he thought he wanted to be a doctor—a chiropractor, to be exact. But when he realized that his money was dwindling and that basic college biology wasn't clicking for him, he left college in his sophomore year and went into sales. He felt that if he worked hard, he could build a good life step by step. In fact, he created an astonishing life.

Even for someone who has grown up in a loving home, life can be hard and success elusive. Tony's story begs the question: Where did a disadvantaged young man get the moxie to conquer the world of business? How did he become so successful with so few resources to start with? Part of the answer is simple: in spite of his tough beginnings, he wanted more out of life, and that desire paved the way for success. But Tony knew that he needed to makes changes if he was to get where he wanted to go. Success requires a conscious decision to do and be something more. That sort of determination, belief, and vision accepts no excuses, has no backup plan, and sees the goal and goes for it. That's what Tony and his twin brother Mike did. They set their sights on the dream of a better life, and they went for it. Nonetheless, at first their vision was relatively modest.

When the brothers were very young and living with the Detroit family who raised them, Tony recalls: "I remember riding with Mike in the backseat of the family car. Our dad pulled up in front of a building and went in. We were waiting in the car with our mom when a long black car pulled up beside us. Mike and I looked out the window. We were impressed. That black car was shining and beautiful. We asked, 'What is that?' We'd never seen a car like that before. I remember our mom saying, 'That's a limousine.'

"'Wow, how do you get one of those?' we asked her. She got upset. She said, 'No, no, no. That's the Mafia. They are the only ones with cars like that.'

"'What's the Mafia?' we asked.

"'Bad people,' she told us. 'That's all you need to know. They are bad people.'

"Even at a young age, as I watched my dad on a typical Saturday, sitting there watching sports, I knew he was not happy; it was obvious. He created a painful, tense atmosphere in the home. I recall thinking, 'I'm not going to be like this,' meaning, 'I'm not going to have this kind of life.' I remember realizing that I wanted more. I had already noticed that other people's lives were not as hard as ours, were not so desperate. 'There must be a way,' I thought."

With that realization, something shifted for Tony. "Whatever my parents thought or said, inside I disagreed with them because I knew I didn't want to live that kind of life. I remember thinking, 'If this is what you say, and this is what you do, I'm thinking and doing the opposite.' When they said, 'We're poor,' I knew that did not mean me. I was sure Mike and I were going to be different—that we *could* be different. I thought, 'Well, okay, I'm not like you. I'm not going down this road. I am not going down your road. I'm going to do something about it.'

"In our house, life felt stressful, as if we were always walking on eggshells. I remember in high school seeing other families that were happier. The parents in those families seemed more relaxed, more in control. They were actually nice. They were more positive. And I also realized that other families didn't abuse their kids and put their kids down. I saw the way other families interacted. And that's when I started recognizing that the way I was being talked to and treated was not normal."

Tony and his twin became co-conspirators. "Mike and I became class clowns. That's the way we would try to get noticed, to get attention, and to overcome our lack of confidence." It was also a way to reject the negativity around them. Tony admits, "I was intimidated by anybody, because I had no confidence whatsoever. I was scared, not knowing what I was going to do." But with the first small, internal step of turning away from their parents' attitudes, the two brothers started to find what they wanted in life and move toward it. Despite his low confidence, Tony was determined to find his way.

With that shift in consciousness, Tony began to observe and understand the people around him in a new way. This, in turn, helped him to understand himself and his life better. "I remember one Saturday being invited onto my friend's dad's boat. My friend had a younger brother. While we were on the boat, the little brother dropped the anchor on his dad's foot by accident. I'll never forget it: as soon as he dropped the anchor, I stood back and tensed up, thinking, 'Uh-oh, someone's going to get his ass kicked.' With his eyes wide open, obviously restraining himself, the father managed to say calmly, 'You know, Chris, that hurt. Please slow down.' That was a huge moment for me. I said to myself, 'You know, if that had been my father, I would have been punched in the face, knocked over, yelled at, and ridiculed.' That was one of the first times I actually digested that maybe I didn't deserve the treatment I got at home. I realized that what was happening in my home was not my fault.

ROLE MODEL EXERCISE

- Think of a person you admire.
- Hold that person in your mind and ask yourself: what makes this person admirable?
- Then ask: what would I do differently if I had this trait?
- Practice applying the trait in your daily life.

"You know, I loved my parents, but at some point I realized I didn't like them," Tony tells me. "And as I watched what happened on the boat that day, I thought, 'Okay, this is a different kind of father.' That family was a good, solid family who interacted positively. I realized it was time to climb out of the hole I was in."

With Tony's determination and openness to find a different way to live, help from a variety of sources showed up along the way. "My friend's father shared some personal growth books and tapes with me, and I started studying all about success. These books all said that you have to retrain your mind. What you think is what you are, and what you believe is what you're going to have. That saved me. That turned the *Titanic* around.

"I knew I wanted to be successful, because it would give me freedom. I knew I had to get out of the place I was in. Growing up, I felt like my childhood was a kind of imprisonment. Childhood is supposed to be fun, but it was rarely fun. I could see that to be successful meant you could have your freedom. If you have enough money, you can do whatever you want. That was my personal motivation, my dream. I wanted freedom."

At first, Tony's and his brother Mike's path to prosperity was about letting go of negativity and figuring out how they could be different from their family and true to their own desires. It took some time—and many more experiences—for Tony to gain a greater sense of self-worth and to achieve fulfillment. But his strong desire to stay true to his vision and to learn how he could become the person he wanted to be never failed.

If we are afraid to follow our own hearts, to take risks and even fail at times—if we are afraid to let go of the old and the familiar—we might miss a chance at true prosperity.

Letting Go of the Old

Interestingly, Marcus and Tony have something else in common besides their happy outcomes: both had to learn to let go of expectations for their lives that didn't belong to them. In order to follow his path and find personal fulfillment, Marcus had to move away from his father's expectation and hope that he would join the family business. Tony also had to move away from family expectations—in his case, expectations of a life of extreme limitation. Finding the courage to simply figure out what they wanted and to pursue it is another common thread.

I was learning from both these men that if we are afraid to follow our own hearts, to take risks and even fail at times—if we are afraid to let go of the old and the familiar—we might miss a chance at true prosperity. We might also miss the opportunity to find out who we are and what we can accomplish. We must be willing to let go of the old judgments, opinions, and worn-out attitudes that limit us. Change requires taking stock and recognizing our own creative responsibility. If we stay stuck in old concepts and do not take action, we may seek vicarious fulfillment or comforts. But they will never have the sweet taste of success, and they will never fill the heart. Eventually we may find ourselves regretting what we could have done if only we'd been willing to move beyond the comfort of the familiar. When we let go of our old expectations and self-image, we make room for a new and expanded expression of our true selves and values.

We can create a life in which we can prosper by staying conscious of who we are and what we really want. This requires following an internal compass based on our genuine selves and our broader goals. To find that internal compass, we must reflect on and acknowledge the personal values that we hold dear.

Your Spark of Individuality

Prosperity can, and must, encompass the unique set of values and goals that define your individual dreams. Henry Ford has some wisdom on this point: "All Fords are exactly alike," Ford said, "but no two men are just alike. Every new life is a new thing under the sun; there has never been anything just like it before, never will be again. . . . [Everyone] should look for the single spark of individuality that makes him different from other folks and develop that for all he is worth. Society and schools may try to iron it out of him; their tendency is to put it all in the same mold, but I say don't let that spark be lost; it is your only real claim to importance."[7]

Self-Esteem and Its Influence on Wealth

What lies behind us and what lies before us are tiny matters compared to what lies within us.

—Henry David Thoreau

The day Tony Cupisz saw that shining black limousine, he began to realize that he wanted something different for his life. He had not yet found his dream, but by taking small steps, he started to climb out of the hole of negativity and low expectations that life had presented to him. He started to change his life.

The Road to Freedom

"I wanted more. I wanted freedom," Tony explains. He knew that would mean having a career. When he left school, he began to look for a path that interested him and that could earn him a good living. He had heard of the concept of residual income from a friend's dad who was in insurance sales.

"I loved that idea—the work you do now continues to pay in the future," Tony explains. "My friend's dad was successful, and I wanted this thing I'd heard him talk about. I thought the concept was great. You sold health insurance to companies and helped them save money, and you received a small percentage each month. I really liked the thought of getting a check every month for work I had done once—you do it one time, and you get paid over and over." Tony laughs when he recalls, "I didn't even know what health insurance was at the time, but I liked the sound of it. Residual income represented freedom." A seed was planted. Years later, Tony and his brother Mike would build their futures and their fortunes on the concept of residual income.

Tony asked his friend's father if he could work for him. With the dad's assent, Tony got his start in sales. He got a desk and a phone, and he went to work selling insurance on straight commission. Now he had not only a job, but a mentor. "I was 19 years old, and I was at a very low point in my life: no money, no prospects—not good at all. My friend's dad lent me a series of audiotapes by Tom Hopkins called *How to Master the Art of Selling*. He gave them to me to teach me how to be a salesman.

"This tape series was a combination of motivation and sales instruction. It teaches how to control a conversation, how to answer questions, how to present. On the very first tape, the first thing Tom Hopkins said was, 'I was 19 years old, I was depressed, and I was broke.' That was exactly the situation I was in: I was 19, I was depressed, and I was broke! So the minute I heard that, I identified with him, and I started listening to those tapes every moment I could. I listened every day, every day, every day.

"As I listened, I discovered that success was all a matter of your mind. Listening to those tapes was important, because it allowed me to hear a human being actually say, 'You can be better, and here is how.' I really needed that. Right then I started rebuilding myself. I started learning how to be more positive. I was studying the psychology of success and the psychology of wealth, and I was learning about my own potential."

As Tony practiced what he was learning, he found that his confidence grew. Of course, he realized that nothing was going to fall from the sky. He had to do the work and remain open to the possibilities.

"At first, I listened only to that Tom Hopkins series," he said. "It taught me all the basics of communication. And I applied what I was learning. Every day, as I was prospecting and selling, I practiced what I heard on the tapes. When I could talk to a grown man and he listened to me, I started gaining more confidence. Another thing that helped me build my self-esteem was seeing other people who were confident. Simply knowing there were people like that, I thought, 'It can be done.' Next, it was: 'How do I get there?'"

To help him learn how to take his next step toward success, Tony began exploring another tape series, *The Psychology of Achievement* by Brian Tracy.

"The psychology aspect helped me because it was all about how to think and why we think the way we do. I didn't realize it at the time, but those tapes were doing more than teaching me the psychology of success. It was like going to a psychologist. It enabled me to understand my whole life and why I felt the way I did. I suddenly realized that throughout my life, the wrong stuff had been going into my brain, and I could change that. I understood that I was talking to myself negatively, rather than how I should be talking to myself, with positive statements. I started changing the way I was thinking and the things I did. I listened until I could almost repeat the entire tape series. And I continued to apply what I learned every day."

Tony was so excited about his discoveries that he wanted to share them. "Every day, I would tell my friends, 'You've got to hear this stuff. We can actually be successful. We can actually do this.' And my friends would laugh at me, because here I was, a 19-year-old listening to motivational tapes. They told me to shut up and put music on. They called me Aristotle, making fun of me because I was listening to this philosophical stuff."

But through the tapes and books, Tony was surrounding himself with personal coaches. "The other things I read that helped me were *How to Win Friends and Influence People*, by Dale Carnegie, and Napoleon Hill's book, *Think and Grow Rich*. Those four authors helped me with a combination of motivation, positive thinking, and communication skills—how to listen, how to talk, how to relate to people better. They gave me something I could use every day. And it worked. Step by step, I started to climb out of the hole. It saved my life."

Tony's friends had—perhaps inadvertently—gotten it exactly right. If Aristotle were alive today, he just might be making motivational tapes of his own. As this wise man said in the fourth century BC, "First have a definite, clear, practical idea—a goal, an objective. Second, have the necessary means to achieve your ends—wisdom, money, materials, and methods. Third, adjust all your means to that end."

A QUESTION

What was the last inspiring book you read, CD you listened to, or movie you watched about someone's success?

How Do We Create Self-Esteem?

Perhaps more than anyone else I spoke to in the course of writing this book, Tony was revealing that, at its heart, the psychology of wealth is a psychology of self-esteem and self-respect. While our culture often considers wealth to be the accumulation of money and assets, true wealth and prosperity hinge on these important psychological intangibles. Fortunately, the steps that we must take to create a prosperous life are most likely the very ones that will ultimately create self-esteem, self-worth, and self-respect. Tony's daily practice—putting into action these powerful ideas that were new to him—was critical to his success. By the way, as we'll learn later, there's even more to Tony's story. And the twists and turns to come have more to add to an understanding of the psychology of wealth.

How exactly are self-esteem and self-worth created? Far too often, money has a disproportionate influence on our sense of self-worth. People frequently believe that if they could somehow acquire more money or more assets, they would feel wealthy. Some believe, for example, that if they received a raise, they would finally feel good about themselves. An individual with this notion who has struggled financially or has failed to meet a financial goal may feel diminished. Over the years, I've seen this struggle in some of my clients—including affluent ones. They feel that something inside them is missing, and that if they only had a bigger house or could afford a more expensive school for their children, they would at last gain entrance to the charmed circle of the truly okay. Yet with each new purchase or rise on the ladder of worldly esteem, the inner void remains unfilled. Although it may seem paradoxical, beliefs like these hold us back from prosperity and prevent us from achieving our highest potential.

It is easy to associate a sense of belonging, worthiness, and security with financial success. Our society both shouts and whispers this association, from the heights of the Fortune 500 list to the depths of our collective psyche. When we know that we can meet our basic financial needs, some types of personal uncertainty are definitely eased. But eventually we discover that simply having a lot of money does not provide inner security or a sense of worthiness. While money helps many things, it has little long-term impact on our self-worth.

Psychologist and wealth counselor Szifra Birke observes, "Money tends not to solve personal problems; money solves money problems."[1] Birke also reports that many financially wealthy people are actually burdened by a vague sense that they don't deserve what they have. Our view of our worthiness seems to hinge in part on how we came by our financial gains and whether we have worked for them in incremental steps. Feelings of unworthiness are especially common in folks who suddenly or unexpectedly come into a large sum of money, such as through an inheritance (or, as we've seen, through a lottery win). They commonly experience "sudden wealth syndrome"; with the acquisition of financial riches, they feel lost and overwhelmed. If you base your self-worth on whether you have reached a particular rung on the ladder to wealth, and if you define wealth by the things you have, an endless loop of dissatisfaction and self-defeat may be the result.

It would be difficult to create financial wealth or any measure of true success without having an intact core sense of self. If you believe that having money will bestow on you a sense of self-worth, you will be caught in a classic Catch-22 loop in which self-esteem must be preceded by wealth, but wealth is possible only if you have self-esteem. Indeed, financial wealth does not automatically confer either self-esteem or self-respect. On the contrary, self-esteem and self-respect seem to be prerequisites for achieving a life of true wealth and prosperity.

The psychology of wealth is a psychology of self-esteem and self-respect.

The Immune System of Consciousness

Self-esteem is a fundamental human need. We simply cannot thrive without it. When we have a solid sense of self-esteem, we feel strong and confident of our ability to cope with life's challenges, and we are able to function at a high level, with a sense of control over our lives. We can expect a measure of success because we know we are capable of being effective.

Psychologist Nathaniel Branden describes self-esteem as a vital combination of two qualities: self-confidence and self-respect. Indeed, self-respect may be the most essential component of self-esteem. With self-respect, we see ourselves as being worthy and deserving of happiness, achievement, and love. Branden says, "I think of self-esteem as the immune system of consciousness. A healthy immune system doesn't guarantee you'll never become ill, but it does reduce your susceptibility to illness and can improve your odds for a speedy recovery if you do get sick. The same is true psychologically. Those with strong self-esteem are resilient in the face of life's difficulties."[2] People who are comfortable with themselves and their achievements take pleasure in being who they are. They face each new challenge with a few deep breaths and a measure of confidence that they'll succeed. As they achieve each new goal, their self-respect grows—and, with it, the ability to fulfill their potential.

When our basic human needs for self-esteem and self-respect are not met, we give up easily, blame others, strive for less, and often fail to achieve our goals. Arrogance, self-righteousness, manipulation, and boastfulness actually betray low self-esteem, primarily in extraverts. Such behaviors are futile attempts to compensate for a sense of unworthiness. Other signs of low self-esteem are a tendency to criticize oneself heavily and to habitually feel dissatisfied with one's performance. For introverts, poor self-esteem may be manifested as an excessive desire to please others and a reluctance to say no out of fear of causing displeasure. Because of an exaggerated fear of making mistakes, people who lack self-esteem avoid taking risks. These unfortunate tendencies sabotage success, acting like internally constructed obstacles to achieving a fulfilling and prosperous life.

In short, creating a psychology of wealth requires a hardy and healthy sense of self-esteem. With it comes a willingness to put oneself on the line and make whatever efforts and stretches are necessary in order to move forward.

One Step at a Time

What if you don't have the self-esteem required to create the life you want? This is where the good news comes in—for the steps that we must take to achieve prosperity are the same steps that increase and strengthen our confidence and self-worth. Indeed, the process of creating a prosperous and successful life is actually the same process that is needed to build self-esteem—one step at a time and one goal at a time.

Robert Reasoner is someone who knows a thing or two about self-esteem. Past president of the National Association for Self-Esteem,[3] he is a former school administrator and the developer of a model for measuring and building self-esteem that has been adopted by schools throughout the United States. Reasoner asserts that true self-esteem "comes from accomplishing meaningful things, overcoming adversity, bouncing back from failures, assuming self-responsibility, and maintaining integrity." He continues, "Some have referred to self-esteem as merely 'feeling good' or having positive feelings about oneself." This incomplete understanding, he says, has stemmed from some popular but incomplete strategies for building self-esteem that include heaping children with praise that isn't based on accomplishment. "Any efforts to build self-esteem," Reasoner says, "must be grounded in reality." It is not possible to grant another person an authentic and durable sense of self-esteem—it is a quality that we gain through our own experiences.

It is not possible to grant another person an authentic and durable sense of self-esteem—it is a quality that we gain through our own experiences.

As Tony Cupisz's experience demonstrates, another effective way to build self-esteem is by raising our awareness of how we think and by making a conscious habit of replacing negative language with positive language when thinking and speaking about ourselves and others. Surrounding oneself with positive messages and with successful and happy people are powerful methods for increasing one's sense of self-worth.

Simply by being alive, we are worthy. If our sense of self is damaged, battered, or fragile, it can be strengthened. Self-esteem is something that we can learn and build upon. And one of the best ways to learn it is by *doing*. The way to create self-esteem in ourselves is through accomplishments. When we accomplish something that is even somewhat difficult, creative, or challenging, we demonstrate to our harshest critics—ourselves—that we are capable. These accomplishments can be small. Yet as long as we realize them, even if we occasionally fall on our faces in the process, we experience our own capacity to achieve and to develop inner strength and tenacity. Going through this step-by-step process is the most powerful thing we can do to build our own self-esteem and self-respect.

In fact, occasional failures and stumbles may be among our best teachers on the path to self-esteem. Many studies, specifically in the past decade, have shown the potentially strengthening effects of adversity. Human beings have an innate resiliency that can turn challenges and setbacks into opportunities for growth. That is why it is so important that we do not beat ourselves up at any point on the path to success and prosperity. We can and must learn from our mistakes and missteps. Turning setbacks and adversity into lessons is one of the most powerful ways to speed progress toward a goal, to gain the strength to carry on, and to create a better life.

Walt Disney exemplifies this principle. A constant innovator, Disney brought an exceptional vision to his work that changed world culture forever. Among many other honors, this beloved icon won 26 Academy Awards, was awarded a Congressional Gold Medal, and had a Los Angeles concert hall named for him. Yet he admitted that his life was riddled with crushing setbacks, disappointments, financial failures, and occasional bouts of depression. His conclusion? "All the adversity I've had in my life, all my troubles and obstacles, have strengthened me," he declared. "You may not realize it when it happens, but a kick in the teeth may be the best thing in the world for you."

Although we don't want to invite adversity into our lives, we can learn a great deal from it, especially when we have the support of strong family and community bonds. In 2000, Glen H. Elder and Rand D. Conger looked at data from several Iowa counties to see how the catastrophic farm crises of the 1980s and 1990s had affected children growing up in rural areas.[4] They found that the majority of these kids were academically successful and had established paths to significant life achievement. Their hardships may actually have strengthened their ability to move forward.

Interestingly, among the resources that helped these challenged kids develop into successful adults were strong, positive bonds with their parents, being required to do productive work, and a family emphasis on "nonmaterial goals." These children had learned that what was most valuable in life transcended money. They had also discovered their own value by facing and accomplishing challenging tasks—one of the most powerful ways to build, strengthen, and empower a sense of personal esteem and self-respect.

> *Trust yourself. Create the kind of self that you will be happy to live with all your life. Make the most of yourself by fanning the tiny, inner sparks of possibility into flames of achievement.*   —Foster C. McClellan

Wild Child

In her mid-twenties, my friend Lennie Alzate had no idea what she wanted to do with her life. Raised in Las Vegas, Nevada, she had been a "hell-raiser" in her teens, according to her mom, but one with an irrepressible curiosity and a thirst for knowledge. Now, with a bachelor's degree in psychology, Lennie was floundering. "What next?" she wondered. Always passionate about reading, she had discovered a fascination with the law and considered becoming a lawyer. But her self-image was still colored by her having been a bit of a "wild child." This seemed incongruous with her notion of what it would take to be an attorney. She had thought a law career was out of her reach, but now that she was an adult and was going nowhere, she reconsidered. "Maybe a law career is possible," she thought. "Why not at least apply to law school? If I can get in, I'll take it from there."

To her amazement, she was accepted at one of the schools she was most hoping to attend. That hurdle passed, she took the next step: she applied for a significant loan and scraped together a few other resources to pay for tuition and to buy her books. She reasoned, "Even if I don't become a lawyer, I'll learn, and I'll be better prepared to make my way in life."

I met Lennie shortly after she had graduated from law school. She was studying for the bar exam, and her focus and determination shone like her infectious smile. I saw that this young woman exemplified the principle that confidence and self-esteem are built one step at a time. Shortly thereafter, she told me that her determination and application had paid off—she'd passed the bar exam on her first attempt. Only 10 percent of her classmates had achieved this feat. Now newly licensed, she became one of a countless number of lawyers who were without a job and hoped to find one. However, her growing confidence in her own ability to have a successful law career had taken a tremendous leap.

At first, Lennie struggled just to survive and had to take odd jobs to get by. She washed cars, worked as a temporary employee in the offices of other attorneys, and performed work that was far beneath her qualifications. Yet she grew stronger in the process. Lennie saw herself as moving forward, one step at a time, despite her apparently slow start. She stayed positive. In spite of her disappointments and financial struggles, she kept going and did her best. She had no idea how success would come, but she had shown herself that she could take on a challenge and overcome obstacles. Her trust in herself—built step by step by doing whatever it took and stretching herself just beyond her comfort zone—was only continuing to grow.

After many months of working at unfulfilling jobs, Lennie received an opportunity that fit more closely with her education and desire. She was asked to join the staff of a successful but small real estate law firm. For months she wrote briefs and learned more about the business. The firm's partners soon recognized her talent and drive. Within a year of their hiring her, she was promoted to lead attorney, and her employers set up a corporation in her name. A mere two years after passing the bar exam, Lennie had a full roster of law clients and was the owner of a new corporation. She had achieved her dream and was doing work that she valued, while enjoying a comfortable income.

Although she had few financial resources, Lennie had decided to roll the dice on her interest in the law. She hadn't known exactly how it would pan out. Moving forward meant putting her self-doubt on the shelf for a while and placing one foot in front of the other in the direction of her goal. Along the way, she had discovered a strong and capable young woman who inspired her to keep going. That young woman happened to be herself.

Investing in Ourselves

While the self-esteem required to achieve true prosperity may seem to have little to do with material possessions, sometimes a well-thought-out and wisely selected purchase can help to boost our self-esteem. This might mean buying a new suit for a job interview, taking out a well-considered loan to buy a more reliable car, or upgrading one's computer to expand one's capacity to serve customers. When these kinds of investments are thoughtfully approached and consciously made, they can increase one's self-esteem and self-respect. Part of the value of such investments is that when we project worthiness and success—whether it is through our attire, our attitude, or the tools we use—the world responds to us in kind. This feedback from our environment can reinforce our self-confidence and inspire continued confidence from others.

When I was growing up, my grandfather Guy demonstrated the value of investing in attire. It is one of the simplest, yet most powerful ways we can project a positive image and feel good about ourselves. It was my grandfather's habit to buy the best clothes he could afford. I recall the many well-tailored suits and ties he wore. Whenever he left his house, he made an effort to look his best. I have no doubt that, as an African American school principal in 1960s Tennessee, he did this deliberately—and to great effect. He was well known and respected in his mixed-race community and was elected to the county board of education. His competence, intelligence, and natural self-confidence won him that seat, but his desire to look the part sure didn't hurt.

Sour Note Turns Sweet

Another key factor in establishing self-esteem and self-worth is to find an avenue for the expression of something you love. Love is expansive, attractive, and cohesive. Here again, one of the most publicly successful people in America, Donald Trump, has wisdom to offer. He asserts that having passion for your work is a key to achieving true wealth. "If you love what you do, you are going to work harder, you are going to try harder, you are going to be better at it, and you're going to enjoy your life more," he writes. "Many people believe that I started out with a lot of money from my father. The truth is that when I started out in business, I was practically broke. My father didn't give me much money, but what he did give me was . . . the simple formula for getting wealthy: work hard doing what you love."[5]

When I was an undergraduate in college, I had a friend whom I will call Nathan who loved to sing. Whenever my friends and I rode in Nathan's car, he would turn on the radio and sing along with popular tunes. The problem was that he wasn't very good at it. My friends and I soon grew tired of listening to his off-key efforts and complained all the way. Finally, we chose to stop riding with him. We would occasionally see him driving around campus, singing his heart out tunelessly, but with gusto. After about a year of refusing the pleasure of Nathan's serenades, there came a day when it happened to be convenient for us to catch a ride with him. As usual, Nathan had the radio playing, and when a popular song started, he began to sing along. We were astounded. Nathan could now deliver the song just as well as the singer who had recorded it. He could see that we were stunned—and impressed—with the skill he had developed. When the next song came on, we asked to hear more of his spectacular voice. Knowing that we had previously stopped riding with him to avoid his singing, he grinned and refused to oblige us with another song. Denying us was his sweet revenge.

Through his love of singing and his relentless practice, Nathan had transformed his voice. Shortly after he surprised us in the car, he became the lead singer in a popular local band that played on and off campus. On several occasions, I saw him perform to large crowds with a stunning display of virtuosity and to screams of approval from the audience. Later, he and his band won acclaim on a tour of the United States. Nathan was well aware that his friends had thought he had no talent. We believed, as most people do, that singing is a talent that you either have or don't have. But he had believed in himself and persisted, practicing daily to no one but his dashboard and his shower curtain. With each passing week, he could hear the improvement in his own voice, and his trust in himself and his own ability grew. Using the tool of his voice and much practice, he developed a skill until it became a talent. Through Nathan, I learned that self-confidence, persistence, and loving what you do can fuel the farthest journey to a cherished goal, as far-fetched as it may seem.

You've got to find what you love. And that is as true for your work as it is for your lovers. Your work is going to fill a large part of your life, and the only way to be truly satisfied is to do what you believe is great work. And the only way to do great work is to love what you do. If you haven't found it yet, keep looking. Don't settle. As with all matters of the heart, you'll know when you find it. And, like any great relationship, it just gets better and better as the years roll on. So keep looking until you find it. Don't settle.

— Steve Jobs, June 12, 2005,
Stanford University Commencement Address

Small Steps

SUCCESS magazine publisher Darren Hardy is an eloquent proponent of the "small steps" principle. He has put the idea into action in his own life, and he has seen it in the lives of the many successful people he's come to know through his work. He says, "Once you start tracking your life, your attention will be focused on the smallest things you're doing right, as well as the smallest things you're doing wrong. And when you choose to make even the smallest course corrections consistently, over time, you'll begin to see amazing results. But don't expect immediate fanfare. When I say 'small' course corrections, I'm talking truly invisible. Chances are no one's going to notice them anytime soon. There will be no applause. No one's going to send you a congratulations card or a trophy for these disciplines. And yet, eventually, their compounding effect will result in an exceptional payoff."

As someone whose life is focused on success every day, Darren has learned this lesson so well that he can spend an entire hour discussing it with an audience and not lose their interest for even a moment: "It's the littlest disciplines that pay off over time, the effort and preparation for the great triumph that happened when no one was looking. And yet the results are exceptional. A horse wins by a nose, but gets 10 times the prize money. Is the horse 10 times faster? No, just a little bit better. But it was those extra laps around the track, the extra discipline in the horse's nutrition, or the extra work by the jockey that made the results a little bit better with compounded rewards."[6]

You have brains in your head.
You have feet in your shoes.
You can steer yourself in any direction you choose.
You're on your own.
And you know what you know.
YOU are the guy who'll decide where to go.
> —Dr. Seuss, *Oh, the Places You'll Go!*

Pioneering psychologist Abraham Maslow asserted that self-esteem allows us to face life with more confidence, benevolence, and optimism. It makes us willing to aim a little higher and stretch a little farther, to take the risks that are necessary if we are to achieve our goals. To develop self-esteem is to expand our capacity to be happy. Moreover, it is only when we have self-esteem and self-respect that we can realize our full potential—

that we can become who we are and all we are capable of becoming, emotionally, creatively, and spiritually. Each step along the way—each small goal achieved, each bruised attempt to jump higher in life, and each debt repaid—teaches us about ourselves and our abilities, and paves the way to success and prosperity, however we define those things for ourselves.

SIGNS OF HIGH SELF-ESTEEM

You

- Learn from your mistakes.
- Are open to other points of view.
- Trust your own judgment.
- Take responsibility for your actions.
- Live in the present.
- Accept others' differences gracefully.
- Know your strengths and weaknesses.
- Accept challenges and take risks.
- Feel grateful for what you have.
- Don't fear change.
- Trust your ability to solve problems.
- Are willing to ask for help.
- Are proactive.
- Persevere and achieve your goals.
- Are unafraid to speak honestly.

SIGNS OF LOW SELF-ESTEEM

You

- Are hypersensitive to criticism.

- Cannot forgive yourself for your mistakes.

- Blame others for your circumstances.

- Feel like a victim; often feel guilty.

- Criticize others frequently.

- Boast about your accomplishments.

- Feel inferior or superior to others.

- Avoid taking risks.

- Fear change and feel anxious.

- Say yes just to please others.

- Have difficulty making decisions.

- Focus on the past or worry about the future.

Evaluating Your Self-Esteem

Here is a simple exercise that requires nothing more than your time, a pen and a pad of paper, and a little bit of reflective honesty. Do you wonder why I'm not suggesting using a computer, an electronic tablet, or some similar device? The reason is simple: writing on paper requires a little more coordination between your head, your heart, and your hand.

1. *Create your four personal lists*

    - Write down your 10 best qualities.

    - Write down 10 things you would like to improve about yourself. *(continues)*

(continued)

- Write down the 10 things that are most important to you.

- Write down your 10 greatest challenges.

2. *Review your lists.* Compare each answer to the "Signs of Low Self-Esteem" and the "Signs of High Self-Esteem."

3. *Reinforce.* For each answer that indicates high self-esteem, write down one thing you can do to reinforce it.

4. *Improve.* For each answer that indicates low self-esteem, write down what you believe you can do to change it, and how and when you will make that change. Remember, self-esteem is built by taking steps to do something that is challenging, creative, or nurturing.

5. *Act now.* Begin your reinforcement and improvement actions immediately. Do not wait for tomorrow or for the beginning of the week, month, or year. There will be no better time to start than right now.

This exercise will help you evaluate your self-esteem and take steps to enhance it. It will also serve as a way to reflect on your progress, which in itself builds self-esteem.

The Stream vs. the Rock

*In the confrontation between the stream
and the rock, the stream always wins, not
through strength but by perseverance.*

—H. Jackson Brown

Tony Cupisz knows that accepting personal responsibility and having dogged perseverance are sometimes all we have to see us through tough times. A component of a healthy and effective psychology of wealth is taking charge and doing what others can't do for us—and then sticking to a vision and never giving up, no matter what may come. As a cofounder of a thriving international company who is also a great father and loved by many people, Tony has the manner of someone who is thoroughly enjoying his life. Listening to him tell his story feels like an unusual privilege, as though I'm being granted a rare view into a world of remarkable success and prosperity that arose from an unlikely beginning.

At one time, Tony Cupisz simply could not catch a break—from the moment he was born, as it turns out. "When my twin brother Mike and I were born," he begins, "we were premature.

Forty-five years ago, premature babies didn't make it as often as they do today. When Mike and I were born, I came out first. I was blue and not breathing, and very sickly looking. The doctor said, 'Just let him go.'

"I met the doctor when I was an adult, so I got the story directly from him and my biological mother. You know how most mothers' eyes light up when they see their newborns? Well, even my mother recalled that when she saw me, she just looked away, thinking, 'Oh my God.' But then the nurse discovered that Mike was on his way. No one had known my mom was carrying twins. Our heartbeats were synchronized, so only one had been heard. According to the doctor, we were his first set of twins, and he didn't want to lose his first set. So he went all out to save us.

"As I was listening to the doctor tell the story, I remember thinking, 'Wait a minute. You mean you went all out only after you learned we were twins? Were you just going to let me go?' When the doctor told me the story, maybe it just came across wrong, but I remember thinking, 'Why wouldn't you go all out to save *any* child?' Anyway, we were both very small. We were put in incubators and needed help to keep our hearts beating. We also needed surgery. It wasn't looking good. On the positive side, of course, we survived!"

Tony and Mike survived, but their early years were exceptionally hard. "When my sister Annette was three, and Mike and I were just two years old, our mother abandoned us on the steps of the trailer where we were living. Our father and mother were divorced, and we had been living alone with our mom in Arizona. She left us sitting there asking her not to leave. As we watched her jump on the back of a motorcycle with a guy and wave good-bye, our last words were, 'Don't leave, Mom.' Many years later, when my mom was asking us for forgiveness, she said it broke her heart leaving us that day and seeing us cry. But still, she left.

"How the neighbors knew to contact our family back in Detroit is unclear, but they contacted them to come and get us. We were living in Arizona because of my mom's asthma; it was supposed to be healthier for her there. My dad, who was very young, had recently gotten home from the service and was on his own, back in Detroit. He couldn't get any help from his family, so we were placed with my mother's relatives. An aunt took in my sister and eventually adopted her. This aunt knew a hairstylist who at the time was unsuccessfully trying to have children. When she was getting her hair done one day, she asked, 'Would you be open to adopting these kids? I have twin boys who need a home,' and she showed her our picture. And so the hairdresser and her husband adopted us." The families agreed that the twins would not see their sister Annette again until they were 18 years old.

Amazingly, Tony and Mike's difficulties were only beginning. Tony continues, "Unfortunately, the circumstances of our upbringing were not good, especially with our adoptive father. He was abusive. He told us that we were losers and that we were stupid and would never amount to anything. That's what he told us all the time. We were made to feel guilty for everything. There was constant guilt about how they didn't have any money, how we were lucky to live in that house, how we were lucky to have the life we did. He'd smack us around and hit us with a belt. It was mental, emotional, and physical abuse.

"The family never had a lot of money, and complaining about money was a constant. Everything was about money. Our adoptive parents were both very stressed out about that. They would call us poor, but I didn't know what they meant. When you're a little kid, you don't understand that being rich or poor has anything to do with money. You just begin to notice that when you go to someone else's house, it's cleaner. The other kid's bedroom is a lot cooler; he has a nice bike and clothes. You get these clues.

Then you want something nice and you can't have it. Then some kid will say something mean to you, and you're shocked. You start feeling separated from other kids, and you start understanding what it means to be poor.

"Somehow, although we didn't have money, I never actually felt poor. I loved my parents, but when I was growing up, I did not like them. If they represented being poor, I rejected it. I wanted to be whatever they were not. I didn't want to be poor. They talked about success as though you just can't have it. Don't count on it; it's not possible—that was the message we heard.

"But that's not how I felt. I feel the same way now that I used to feel—that if I worked really hard and was ambitious and wanted to have good things happen to me, I could. Somehow I could. I realized early on that success was about making choices and that I was responsible for those choices. That's all Mike and I had—the choices we made. I think having each other also helped our resilience."

Despite the difficult family life, abuse, and lack of financial security that faced the twins, the two understood that if they were to move beyond their adoptive parents' lifestyle, they had to do things differently.

"So I worked hard. I tried everything. And good things did happen to me. I always believed that everyone else could do the same thing. Now I believe that success is achievable if people *choose* it and work toward it. I also believe that what you seek is what you get. And there are sometimes circumstances that help you or hinder you, but I believe you should still keep looking for a path that lets you move forward. If you want success, you have to keep moving ahead, regardless of the obstacles that stand in your way. Success is not going to come to you if you don't fight for it. You can't try something and say it doesn't work just because it did not work *yet*. For me, it's about never quitting. You should never quit."

Success is not going to come to you if you don't fight for it. You can't try something and say it doesn't work just because it did not work yet. For me, it's about never quitting. You should never quit. —Tony Cupisz

With maturity comes the possibility for growth and change in our relationships. As adults, Tony and Mike reconciled with their adoptive father and healed many of the wounds of the past. With their reconciliation has come forgiveness and peace. As Tony explains, "Today our adoptive father is proud of us and has become a good grandfather. People can change and become better if they choose to."

Tony has a magnetism that irresistibly draws others to him. When he speaks, everyone around him is captivated. Knowing that he started farther down in life than most people will ever go and has worked his way up to an exceptionally prosperous life certainly got my attention. After I heard more of his story, it was becoming clear to me that we have more power over our own path to prosperity than we might expect.

Personal Responsibility Is a Conscious Choice

"Everything in your life exists because you first made a choice about something," says *SUCCESS* magazine publisher Darren Hardy. "Choices are at the root of every one of your results. Each choice starts a behavior that over time becomes a habit." In his bestselling book *The Compound Effect*, Darren explains that this effect is the accumulation of all the choices that we make moment by moment, day in and day out, large and small. These choices add up to habits that produce either a prosperous life or a life that is something less than we want it to be.

"In essence, you make your choices, and then your choices make you. Every decision, no matter how slight, alters the trajectory of your life," Darren observes.[1] I agree. Ultimately our lives are a reflection of the conscious and unconscious choices that we make each day. We make many—if not most—of our choices unconsciously. Although we may not intend to sabotage ourselves, by not being fully aware of our decision making, we may find that we have created results that we neither intended nor desire.

To make ourselves more aware, Darren suggests that we ask ourselves: "How many of my behaviors have I not 'voted on'? What am I doing that I didn't consciously choose to do, yet continue to do every day?" These questions capture the mindfulness that is needed if we are to create a prosperous life. By bringing awareness and some deliberation to our decisions, we can make choices that support expansion and true progress. Developing the habit of taking a moment to stop, take a breath, and consider what we're doing and why—as well as what it is we really want—can help us make better choices. Doing this helps keep us from falling into unconscious patterns that may not have served us in the past.

Like the stream that wins over the rock, by moving forward and persisting with the right choices at each bend, we can reach our goals. The strength of the river is gained through momentum, by the focus of the flow in one direction. We can use that momentum to move toward our dreams and our goals.

Sardine Sandwiches

I enjoy a story told by author Brian Tracy. He relates the tale of a construction worker who, on his lunch break, complains loudly and profusely about having a sardine sandwich. To the annoyance of his coworkers, he repeats his complaint about his sardine sandwich every day for the next few days. Finally, one of his coworkers leans over and suggests that he ask his wife to make him something else for lunch. The man replies, "Oh, I'm not married. I make my own lunches!"[2]

The story is funny, but it reminds us to ask ourselves this question: what circumstances in my life am I dissatisfied with (and may gripe about) but do little to change? Sometimes we may feel stuck. But as the masters of our own lives, we have little cause to complain about circumstances that are of our own making. Too often, we place the responsibility for our situation elsewhere and don't change the things that are clearly within our control. Tracy concludes, "The acceptance of personal responsibility is what separates the adult from the child. It's the great leap forward into maturity. Responsibility is the hallmark of the fully integrated, fully functioning human being."

As Tony's story illustrates, creating a life that you value requires accepting the idea that you're completely responsible for yourself. Such a good life also involves the realization that no one is going to come to your rescue—nor, in general, should they. There's very little that you cannot do or have after you accept that "If it's to be, it's up to me."[3] When we assign to others the responsibility for where we are or who we have become, we start to surrender small parts of ourselves. We begin to disconnect ourselves not only from personal responsibility, but from our personal power. If we absolve ourselves of the need to make changes on our own, we reinforce the idea that we lack control over our lives. Our own sense of powerlessness becomes a self-fulfilling prophecy. Accepting responsibility allows us to persist, despite obstacles and setbacks. We become the stream that moves forward despite all the twists, turns, and rocks in our way.

Which Wolf?

A Native American parable captures an important lesson about personal responsibility and making choices. An old Cherokee was teaching his grandson about life. He said, "I feel as if I have two wolves fighting in my heart. One wolf is vengeful, jealous, angry, and violent. The other wolf is loving and compassionate."

The grandson thought about this for a minute and then asked him, "Which wolf will win the fight?" The grandfather replied, "The one I feed."[4]

Whatever we focus our attention on is what we are nurturing in our lives. That attention is reflected in our thoughts, feelings, and actions. Whatever we feed will live, grow, and become real.

How We Respond

We cannot always control the circumstances that we are faced with, but we can choose the way we respond to them. Viktor E. Frankl, the revered Austrian psychotherapist and author, was a Nazi concentration camp survivor who endured imprisonment in Auschwitz. The degradation, brutality, and loss of life that he witnessed was beyond comprehension. Among many other causes for grief and despair, he lost his wife, who died after being transferred to Bergen-Belsen. Yet throughout this ordeal, he persevered and found transcendence. It was from his and others' suffering in the camps that he came to his hallmark conclusion that even in the most absurd, painful, and dehumanized situations, life has meaning. Frankl realized that the meaning in life does not come from what happens to us, but from how we interpret what happens to us—and then, what we do with it.

Viktor Frankl thoughtfully argued that we must accept responsibility for our choices, even the most subtle and internal decisions, including what we think. He himself made conscious choices that profoundly changed the course of his life. In "A Tribute to Viktor Frankl," Paul G. Durbin, Ph.D., recounts Dr. Frankl's decision to stay in Europe in the early 1940s, when he had a chance to escape Nazism and come to America.

The situation in his homeland was becoming more and more difficult for those of the Jewish race. The local Jewish synagogue had been bombed and left in ruins by the Nazis. . . . As the synagogue was destroyed, he went to a nearby Christian church. He prayed that God would give him some direction as to what he should do. He wanted to know if he should go to America or stay with his family. Though he earnestly prayed, no answer came. He left the church feeling that God had ignored him.

On the way home, he came to the destroyed synagogue. He stopped for a few moments and picked up a piece of wood to take home as a keepsake for his father. When he arrived home, he examined the piece of wood more closely. As he read the inscription on the piece of wood, he realized that indeed God had heard his prayer and had answered him. The inscription on the piece of wood read, "Honor your father and mother." His parents were in Europe and could not leave. He stayed in Europe and eventually ended up a prisoner of the Nazis.

If Frankl had not gone to that church, stopped at that destroyed synagogue, picked up that piece of wood and carried it home and read what was inscribed on it; would we have ever heard of Viktor Frankl? Maybe! Would he have had the impact on the second half of the [twentieth] century that he had? I doubt it! He did go by that church, stopped at the destroyed synagogue, picked up that piece of wood, carried it home, read it and become one of the great contributors to psychology. . . .

Frankl survived the Holocaust and the Nazi death camps. . . . Even in the degradation and misery of the concentration camps, Frankl was able to exercise the most important freedom of all: the freedom to determine one's own attitude and spiritual well-being.[5]

Under the most extreme circumstances, in which anyone could feel justified in blaming others for his distress, Dr. Frankl used his experience to help his fellow prisoners and ultimately to develop a new approach to psychotherapy that has helped millions more. His book *Man's Search for Meaning*, written in 1959, remains one of the most widely read volumes in the world.

No matter what situation or challenge we find ourselves facing, we can decide how to respond. We can feel victimized and resigned and give others power over our lives, or we can take personal responsibility for the choices we make. To live a more prosperous life, we must accept responsibility.

You must take personal responsibility. You cannot change the circumstances, the seasons, or the wind, but you can change yourself. That is something you have charge of.

—Jim Rohn

How Did We Get into This Mess?

Today, in the United States and many other countries, our economies are reeling from a global financial crisis. As we work to recover and struggle to pay the bills, much has been said and written about how we got into this mess. How *did* we get here? What happened that allowed our economies to go so far astray, right to the brink of self-destruction? In other words, who is responsible?

We like to say that it was the "bad guys" (Bernie Madoff and his ilk) or the greedy bankers and brokerage firms, abetted by government policies that allowed the worst corporate behavior to emerge and consumers to run amok. All of this is undeniably true. However, just as each life is the sum of both the minute and the major choices that a person makes every day, our collective lives are the product of countless individual contributions. In other words, our national and international pickle is one that is of our own making. Each human being in any of the groups involved—brokers, bankers, investors, regulators, and regular citizens—made individual decisions that added up to a mess of massive proportions. To be sure, some contributed more than others, but in truth, we've gotten here together. If Bernie Madoff hadn't been wicked, many people wouldn't be in their current dire straits. But if we hadn't borrowed excessively on our houses, neither would we.

The big mess came from a lot of individual decisions that accumulated to create it. Paradoxically, that's the good news— because if we can make a mess, that means we can unmake it. We can start to make individual decisions and take individual steps that will strengthen our own financial lives and add up to a righting of our collective ship.

As I pondered what leads to individual prosperity, I wanted to know: What was it that we as individuals may have done to add to the pile of bad debt and financial dysfunction? As we went about our individual lives, doing our individual best to prosper and thrive, was there a point where we went wrong? How did we as individuals make so many financial decisions that were not in our best interests? Surely actions that are not self-enhancing are signs that choices were being made unconsciously. Was it mass hypnosis? No. But something resembling a seduction seems to have been taking place. We are responsible for our own decisions. But I was curious: what factors helped entice us down the path of unconscious borrowing and spending?

Borrowing Undergoes a Metamorphosis

For most people, acquiring wealth has been a matter of moving up by taking small steps in any way one can. Credit has long played an essential role in this process. Consumer credit has allowed generations of people to purchase such things as homes and cars, and to finance higher education—all actions that have materially improved their lives. For most of our history, this credit took the form of installment loans. Even a generation or two ago, it was this kind of loan that allowed people to buy washers, dryers, televisions, refrigerators, vacuum cleaners, and other genuine conveniences of a flourishing life. This budget-conscious form of borrowing required face-to-face discussions between the borrower and the lender on the consumer's needs and means. How did borrowing morph from a transaction that required consultation and deliberation into writing one's own very large check on a home equity line? During the prerecession borrowing spree, these easily written checks were often used to finance "conveniences" such as transforming one's kitchen into a showcase of marble and brushed stainless steel.

When new, easy forms of credit entered the marketplace in the early 1960s, they began to replace the popular installment credit plans, especially for middle- and upper-class citizens. Unlike traditional installment loans, these new, revolving forms of credit—familiar to us now as credit cards and, more recently, home equity lines of credit—did not require repayment within a fixed period. Only minimum payments were required. They also offered the allure of nearly effortless borrowing. Retailers encouraged customers to pay for their wares this way, because they quickly learned that customers who used revolving credit or "charge cards" purchased significantly more than customers who paid cash. Indeed, the average charge sale was three times the average cash sale.[6]

Did consumers' needs suddenly escalate by 300 percent? It's unlikely. A need to borrow may be legitimate. However, when we aren't required to deliberate on the real costs and benefits of a purchase or a loan, the likelihood that the decision will be a thoroughly conscious one diminishes. Simply put, this kind of instantaneous credit encourages unconscious spending. And it challenges our budgetary discipline sorely. The credit card is now the most widely used credit vehicle in the world. With a card in one hand and Internet access in the other, our self-control and discipline are tested at every turn.

They Don't Make It Easy to Just Say No

Understanding the escalation of debt worldwide, and specifically in the United States, also requires a look at how marketing affects our suggestible consumer psyches. In a fascinating report, "Consumer Debt in the U.S.," José D. Roncal explains, "The branding of our world has become one of the major problems linked to consumer debt. Everything is so branded, part of our personal identity has become tied up with the labels and products we choose. A teenage boy walks into an athletic shoe store.

Before he buys anything, he spends a long time just standing there, staring at four walls stocked from floor to ceiling with too many choices. The most pressing question on his mind is not, 'Which one will fit best?' It's certainly not, 'Which one can I afford?' It's most likely, 'Which one is me?'"[7] Add to the mix instant and easy revolving credit, with virtually no time between desire and fulfillment, and you have a perfect formula for escalating debt.

In the 1920s, Edward Bernays, the "father of public relations" and nephew of Sigmund Freud, began to experiment with ways to manipulate public opinion. He was the first to use the psychology of the subconscious and "third-party authorities" to influence behavior in the marketplace. Since then, we consumers have been powerfully influenced by advertising. Roncal asserts that the psychological effects of advertising on the use of credit are nearly irresistible: "Once the suggestion has been planted in the minds of consumers that they are linked to the same habits as others similar to themselves, the marketing mission has been accomplished. It's the same 'wisdom of the crowd' herd mentality that leads to stock bubbles." This is one reason that even when people know that their spending is out of control, it's difficult for them to put the brakes on. "When you throw technology into the mix," says Roncal, "over-spending and debt picks up speed and puts tremendous demands on our self-control."

If we look at the statistics, Edward Bernays's experiments in public manipulation seem to have been highly successful. "Government statistics show online sales grew from $4.6 billion in 1999 to $136 billion in 2007," Roncal reports. Forrester Research, a technology and market research company, projects that U.S. Web sales will climb from the current $200 billion annually to nearly $300 billion by 2015. As Roncal concludes, "If that's the case, we could be clicking our way into astronomical heights of credit card debt!"[8]

Of course, we can't pin all the blame for our sometimes questionable decisions on marketing gurus and ignore our own responsibility. Yet it's apparent that certain types of credit require less thoughtfulness. Every form of credit can be used consciously and responsibly. Any form of borrowing and spending that intrinsically requires time for conscious reflection and a review of one's budget will be most helpful in steering us clear of the rocks in the stream.

Success on any major scale requires you to accept responsibility.... In the final analysis, the one quality that all successful people have is the ability to take on responsibility. —Michael Korda

---

Getting Control of Your Life

Last year, as part of my research, I attended an educational forum and press conference at which consumers shared their strategies for managing in tough times. There I met a career woman named Priscilla. She lives in a small Virginia town, attends church, and loves life. She married young, started working, and did everything she believed was needed to create a pretty nice life. Yet everything fell apart.

Priscilla quietly shared, "I went through a divorce, and that hurt my credit." She paused and then explained what happened next: "And then I lost my job." Already devastated from the breakup of her marriage, now she had poor credit, dwindling finances, mounting debt, and no income. As frequently happens, the divorce set her back emotionally and financially, but over time she persisted. "Eventually," she said, "I found a good job with the State of Virginia."

Even with her new job, her finances were in disarray. She made her next priority climbing out of her financial hole. Like other people who spoke that day, she wasn't sure where to turn. She hadn't wanted to face the problem. It had been easier to let things slide. However, she knew that she needed to make some tough choices, and tackling those choices head-on had become important to her. Priscilla continued, "I went to a consumer finance company near where I live and asked if they could help. I wanted to pay old bills and get my payments into something I could manage. I wanted to rebuild my credit." She was pleased with the process, explaining what happened at the loan office. "We went over my budget carefully. We got all my bills together, and they helped me consolidate everything. They also taught me how to call creditors and handle each debt appropriately.

"It wasn't easy, but facing the situation and getting my finances under control made me feel great," Priscilla told me. "I was able to finally pay bills that had been lingering for years. Since then, my credit score has gone up, and my budget is balanced. I don't live lavishly, but I'm able to purchase things again and move ahead. I was able to get control of my finances and my life." As she stepped away from the podium at the press conference, Priscilla's smile filled the room. People milled around her to congratulate her on her achievement, and I felt pleased for her. I was struck again by the power of taking personal responsibility and bringing consciousness to our financial decisions. It's a big step in creating genuine prosperity.

Back to Tony

Tony Cupisz is not the first person to observe, "Life is not necessarily fair." But he also understands that sometimes progress is made simply by putting one foot in front of the other. "Your circumstances may not be easy," explains Tony. "Mine certainly weren't. You may not know what you're going to do or how you're going to do it. But you have to do something every day. Just do something. Even if it's absolutely what you don't want to do, you have to take steps. It's about taking personal responsibility for your life. To earn money and pay your bills, you may need to take a job that you don't want to take. But then, when you do, you might meet people, and perhaps something will lead you to something else, to something good. Anything can lead you to something new. These are life's stepping-stones."

Tony's observation reminded me of Norman Vincent Peale's wise advice: "Action is a great restorer and builder of confidence. Inaction is not only the result, but the cause, of fear. Perhaps the action you take will be successful; perhaps different action or adjustments will have to follow. But any action is better than no action at all."[9]

Value Is What You Get

Price is what you pay.
Value is what you get.
—Warren Buffett

During the Vietnam War, Bennie Taylor served as a paratrooper in the 173rd Airborne Brigade based in Bien Hoa. He was awarded a Purple Heart for wounds he received in action in March of 1966. As soon as Bennie could walk again, he went right back to combat duty. I heard about Bennie when he took a trip to Kentucky to participate in an event inspired by his unique family history. Now in his sixties, Bennie wearing a dapper fedora brings to mind images of the old blues greats Muddy Waters and T-Bone Walker. His smoky voice evokes the rasp of aging leaves skittering over the ground in an autumn wind, and you can imagine him as a singer with great soul. When asked, sure enough, he says he loves gospel music and sings in the church choir. He's an unassuming man of few words, and he's so friendly and gentle that I'm sure dogs and children can't resist him. His demeanor is that of a storyteller who allows you not only to hear his story, but to feel it. Bennie loves to share the story of his family's role in a legendary bank robbery of the Great Depression—and that's what his trip was all about.

In 1938, Bennie's grandfather on his mother's side, Arthur Mimms, was the mail guard in Guthrie, Kentucky. On January 5, a mail pouch with $25,000 in U.S. currency addressed to the Federal Reserve was being carried on Arthur's shoulder. He had been chosen for the security job because he was an expert marksman with both hands. His daily ritual was to walk mail to and from the train depot. On the day of the robbery, he was joined, as usual, by two other armed guards. But that day was not to be a usual one.

"As my grandfather went through his routine transporting the money to the depot, everything went wrong," Bennie recounted. "As he and the guards headed toward the building, a car sped up to them, and three men piled out. Under their coats they had pistols and submachine guns. There was a burst of machine-gun fire, and they shot my grandfather. He was murdered right on the spot. The sheriff was dropped by three bullets in his legs. After the robbers collected the mail pouch with the money, they hauled the third guard into the car and drove out of the station. A short distance from town, they dumped their hostage and made their getaway.

"The story got national attention, since it was the largest mail robbery in American history up to that time." The postmaster general's annual report that year wrote of Bennie's grandfather: "It is with sadness, and yet with pride, the fact is recorded that Arthur Mimms, colored United States mail messenger at Guthrie, Kentucky, was murdered on January 5, 1938, while defending the mail that was in his custody." An extensive manhunt tracked down two of the robbers, who were both sent to Alcatraz for 55 years on federal charges. The third man, who had murdered Bennie's grandfather, was killed as federal agents attempted to capture him.

The town of Guthrie, of course, was gratified that the gangsters had been brought to justice. Seventy years after the robbery, in 2008, they started a tradition of reenacting the infamous heist every January 5 to honor the brave men who had defended the U.S. mail that day. After the first of these events, word of the reenactment made its way to Bennie's sister, who happens to be the family historian. She contacted the town, which invited Bennie's family to the next reenactment as honored guests. The family was delighted. "It was a personal thing for us," Bennie related. "It's part of our lives, a touching part of our family history, and they were going to include us and acknowledge us at this event. We took it to heart. We felt grateful that they chose to respect and honor our grandpapa. It was to be a large affair for the city and for the family, too."

From California, Indiana, Florida, and North Carolina, various branches of Bennie's family traveled to Kentucky for the event. There was no way Bennie was going to miss it. "I am next to the youngest in a family of 11 children, the 'knee baby,' and it was very important for me to be there," he said. The only hitch was that he didn't have money readily available to cover the expense of traveling. Standing on his own is important to Bennie. It's part of his character, and it has worked well for him. There was no one in the family whom he wanted to ask for assistance, so he took out a small installment loan. "It enabled me to go to this event. And I'll tell you how it made me feel—independent. My independence matters to me."

Bennie is retired now and lives a modest—and, from his point of view, rewarding and prosperous—life. It's rich in experience and travel, and in friends and family. He goes to his high school reunions in Indiana, attends the now-annual family reunions in Guthrie, and visits his remaining siblings from time to time. His strong sense of self-reliance comes in part from knowing that he can take on life's challenges squarely, something he learned from jumping from military aircraft into enemy territory and watching out for his fellow soldiers and himself. To Bennie, the small loan he took out to make his trip to Guthrie brought immense value to his life. Bennie's decision deepened his sense of belonging to his extraordinary family and to his grandfather's legacy.

"Price Is What You Pay. Value Is What You Get."

The qualities that make a life prosperous are both intensely personal and subjective. The experiences that bring meaning and forward momentum to one person's life may be of little importance or value to another. I have also learned that people create meaning in the most fascinating and diverse ways. The stories of what enriches a life can be as varied as the grains of sand in a desert. When viewed from afar, the desert looks like a vast, uniform landscape. When we look more closely, however, we see that each grain of sand is unlike any other.

Although in a very different way from Bennie Taylor's, my own grandfather's life played a key role in my education. He taught me an important lesson about price and value. As a kid, I visited my grandparents at their home outside of Memphis during summer vacations. It was a carefree time in the hot, humid South, with miles of nature to roam and explore. I had access to forests, lakes, and lush, open fields. On occasion I would go hunting or fishing with my grandfather, who exuded a quiet and compassionate sense of authority. Fishing at the crack of dawn was not my favorite outdoor activity. Although I enjoyed my grandfather's company, the fish were usually slow to bite, but the mosquitoes were not. I always ended up itching and scratching for days afterward. At other times, we would go to town to shop or run other errands. Even at that young age, one thing I noticed about my grandfather was that the things he purchased were always of high quality. He bought the best that he could afford, which was not always the least expensive. This wasn't done for show or to impress, but because he understood that value was as important as price, if not more so.

It's a simple formula, but one that we sometimes forget: you get what you pay for.

This philosophy extended to the way he treated other people, and also to what he expected from those with whom he associated. He valued and showed respect to everyone he encountered, regardless of rank or station. A practical man, he expressed a quiet optimism that gave strength to those around him. Honesty was paramount to him. Because of this, people treated him with respect and gave him their best. People in and around Memphis held him in high regard. I have no idea where or how he learned his appreciation for value, but it served him and my grandmother well throughout their lives, and this understanding of value was passed to me as an inherited, unspoken gift. It was simply a part of who they were, and I am blessed to have learned it from them.

It's a simple formula, but one that we sometimes forget: you get what you pay for. But what you pay may not fully represent the value of your purchase to you. Warren Buffett expressed this idea with midwestern plainspokenness when responding to questions about why he wasn't buying stocks whose prices had fallen.

Why, he was asked, wasn't he grabbing up these bargains, the way others were? His answer: "Price is what you pay. Value is what you get."

WHAT THINGS DO YOU CONSIDER MOST IMPORTANT IN MAKING A PURCHASE?

- Price?
- Quality?
- Service?
- The experience?
- Ease and availability?

It is easy to confuse value and price. In general, in our society, items that are highly valued simply cost more. For example, the price of a sapphire ring is many hundreds of times that of a ring made with mother of pearl. The reasons for these differences are both practical and perceptual. Many factors go into determining the price of an object—the rarity of the raw materials or the difficulty of obtaining them; the amount of labor and energy required to manufacture, ship, and sell the object; and so on. Merchants and marketers understand this relationship. They also grasp our assumption (which is often, but not always, correct) that the more valuable something is, the higher its price tag will be. For this very reason, when my friend Robert was trying to sell his successful business but was getting few offers, a savvy marketing associate recommended that he raise his asking price. Robert scoffed. If he hadn't been able to sell the firm at a low price, how could he possibly expect to sell it for more? His associate persisted and eventually talked Robert into giving it a try for just two weeks. Within a week of raising the price, Robert received an offer.

So what makes something truly valuable to us? When we purchase something—or when we choose to buy one product rather than another—many factors come into play. Price is almost never the only consideration, or even the most important one. As my grandfather quietly demonstrated to me many times, value often trumps price. Marketing research confirms his wisdom. Recently, a survey conducted by Retail Eyes, a British customer-experience-improvement agency, showed that fewer than one out of five consumers intended to make purchases based on the lowest price available. Retail Eyes CEO Tim Ogle said, "Customers are subconsciously running value equations throughout their entire experience and that includes more than just price; it includes the whole experience."[1]

Value is also not an absolute. Even the value of money itself doesn't lie in the amount we have; it lies in what we do with it to bring pleasure, meaning, and significance to our lives. True value can be determined only by each of us based on our individual circumstances. Ultimately, you are the only person who can determine whether something has enriched your experience or your life.

In many cases, taking on credit can lead to financial prosperity more quickly than saving for the same investment or purchase.

—Melissa Koide and Rachel Schneider

The Value of Having Options

I have also observed that one of the most important factors in creating a psychology of wealth is the knowledge that one has options. Knowing that we can choose a solution that suits our priorities, needs, and values is not only financially advantageous, but also psychologically empowering. A sense that our options are limited, or that someone else has decided what's best for us, undermines our self-esteem—and with it, our ability to achieve meaningful prosperity. Indeed, a lack of options can be a major cause of distress.

Among the most important sets of options we have are those for borrowing money. Today, entire economies are struggling to deal with debt and with enormous financial stress. Credit and debt have played central roles in the financial troubles that have befallen many individuals and societies. Yet, as I have learned, the use of credit can be a powerful means to create prosperity. Melissa Koide and Rachel Schneider captured this succinctly in a paper for a 2010 Harvard Business School symposium: "Credit can facilitate an investment or purchase that provides the foundation for other wealth-building activities." These wealth-building activities can be surprisingly modest-seeming investments, like repairing a car that enables a worker to take a better-paying job or purchasing a washing machine that, as Koide and Schneider point out, "frees time for childcare or education instead of visits to the Laundromat."[2]

The average running card balance is $8,000. At a 15% interest rate, that balance will, over a lifetime, impoverish the borrower by $60,000 in interest charges. —Forbes[3]

Unpacking Credit

If credit has two faces, I wondered, are certain credit options more conducive to building wealth than others? If credit is both part of the problem *and* a potential tool for prosperity, are there ways in which we can use credit that tip it in one direction or the other? Finding the answer means unpacking the various credit options available to us today and figuring out the impact of each type. Which forms of credit, I wanted to know, might tend to support a sense of financial control, self-determination, and personal responsibility? And which might undermine that sense? Which forms of credit might be more conducive to conscious decision making, goal achievement, and self-esteem? In other words, which forms of credit, if any, might support a psychology of wealth?

A Plastic Nation

One form of credit has become such a staple of modern life that it has earned its own pseudonym: "plastic." In the previous chapter, I discussed some of the pitfalls and benefits of using credit cards. For many of us, this exceptionally convenient form of credit has become a necessity of life. However, as has already been noted, relying on credit cards can lull us into a false sense of prosperity that permits unconscious overspending through impulse buying. Interest rates on credit cards can be relatively low, but the disadvantage of this form of revolving credit is that the interest can compound almost indefinitely, and the inducement of minimum payments encourages the perpetuation of debt. People often end up paying amounts that dwarf the original sums that they borrowed.

Home Equity Lines of Credit (HELOCs)

Another popular form of revolving credit that I touched upon in the previous chapter is home equity lines of credit. They generally offer higher credit limits than unsecured credit cards and even lower interest rates. Interest payments can also be tax-deductible. Yet, in reality, this type of credit is a second mortgage on one's home—renamed and repackaged as HELOCs in a marketing stroke of genius. These credit lines carry the same perils of unconscious overspending as credit cards, and their longer repayment terms can create astronomical levels of long-term debt. Yet the potential benefits of these credit lines have made them attractive to many people.

What other credit options are available to us as ordinary consumers? If we are unable—or unwilling—to borrow from our family and friends, we have several other regulated and legitimate options.

Bank Loans

Among these options are bank loans. Their advantages include relatively low interest rates, fixed interest and principal payments, and fully amortized debt terms. However, banks do not typically offer small dollar loans, because such terms make these loans unprofitable.[4] In addition, the often large loans available from banks require specific types of collateral and can involve a lengthy application process. For most consumers, banks prefer to offer credit cards rather than loans.

Credit Union Loans

Credit unions offer additional lending options. Because credit unions are nonprofit and tax-exempt, their loans may come with more lenient lending terms and lower fees than typical bank loans. However, to qualify for a loan requires membership in the credit union and often the opening of associated accounts. In addition, credit union membership and many credit union accounts carry their own fees and conditions.

Like banks, most credit unions avoid small dollar loans and instead prefer to offer credit cards. Some credit unions with specialized charters, however, can offer small dollar loans at below-market rates. These Community Development Credit Unions (CDCUs) provide financial services primarily to low-income communities. Because of CDCUs' charters and their reliance on taxpayer funding and charitable contributions, membership in a CDCU may be restricted to consumers who meet certain income guidelines.

Traditional Consumer Installment Loans

Another regulated and legitimate credit option is traditional consumer installment loans. These are typically small dollar loans—that is, they range from several hundred dollars to approximately 10,000 dollars (amounts vary from state to state). These loans are relatively simple and easy to obtain. Like several other types of loans, including bank loans, student loans, and car loans, a traditional consumer installment loan must be repaid within a fixed period of time. Unlike some other types of small dollar loans, these traditional loans require no balloon payments and are considered very safe. Interest rates on these installment loans are generally higher than those on other forms of traditional credit. Yet even with a higher annual percentage rate (APR), an installment loan's fully amortized repayment schedule often results in significantly lower interest costs over the life of the loan. Installment loan office hours are convenient, and a hallmark of these finance companies is making personal connections with customers.

As with bank loans and credit union loans, getting a consumer installment loan involves two people sitting face to face having a thoughtful discussion about the consumer's budget and ability to pay, as well as the purpose of the loan. This process inherently requires us as consumers to make borrowing a conscious decision. Unlike with credit cards and home equity lines, the ability to incur instantaneous, unconscious, and nearly endless incremental loans is simply not there.

Main Street Lending

Before I started conducting research for this book, I knew little about consumer installment loans. But as I learned more about their historical role in building wealth—starting with the credit plans introduced by the Singer Sewing Machine Company in the 1800s—they piqued my curiosity and eventually gained my respect. Today, installment loans can be found on the main streets and in shopping malls in most American towns in small offices bearing signs that simply say "Loans." Their users include millions of small business owners, factory workers, computer techs, nurses, members of the military, retirees, and everyone in between. I learned that many parents and grandparents introduce their children and grandchildren to the local consumer finance company in order to establish their credit, improve their credit scores, and achieve their goals. Although traditional consumer finance companies serve millions, many people may pass their small offices every day without even noticing them.

Many parents and grandparents introduce their children and grandchildren to the local consumer finance company in order to establish their credit, improve their credit scores, and achieve their goals.

Supporting a Psychology of Wealth

I could see the value of traditional installment loans for supporting a psychology of wealth. Installment loans encourage the responsible repayment of a debt for a specific goal in a set period of time. They support responsibility in other ways, too. In his book *Financing the American Dream: A Cultural History of Consumer Credit*, Lendol Calder observes, "The installment plan of repayment forces typical credit users to adopt disciplines of money management that would have impressed even Poor Richard. . . . Installment credit imposes on borrowers financial regimens requiring discipline, foresight, and a conscious effort to save income in order to make payments on time."[5]

Repaying a loan in a timely fashion fosters the self-esteem that comes from meeting a challenge responsibly. Interestingly, default and delinquency rates on traditional consumer installment loans are very low. Calder also points out that "95.5 percent of consumer debt gets paid."[6] Installment loans may not seem like the most exciting or trendy way to borrow. However, the responsibility and discipline required to use these loans make them a good fit for fostering a sense of mastery over our own finances.

The Best of Intentions

As I've explored the psychology of wealth—and spoken to finance professors, legislators, consultants, credit counselors, and many individuals who are creating balanced, stable, and thoroughly prosperous lives—I've come to understand that conscious financial decision making and the option to borrow responsibly are essential for creating prosperity. Throughout history, the reputation of debt has gone through many ups and downs. From biblical times to the most recent travails of Wall Street, debt has been an easy target. The role of debt in the recent international economic crisis has understandably led to a call for stronger regulatory safeguards to restrict the practices of lending institutions and other financial services companies. Yet I have come to believe that because of the positive and genuinely life-enhancing role that certain types of loans play, these loans should not be caught in the same net as the unhealthy lending practices that have led to individual and collective financial troubles. These important lending options include standard mortgages, auto loans, credit union loans, bank loans, and traditional installment loans.

One of the most knowledgeable, and downright illuminating, people I have met in the course of researching this book is Harold Black, Ph.D. He is professor emeritus and James F. Smith, Jr. Professor of Financial Institutions at the University of Tennessee.

From Dr. Black and others, I learned about recent moves by state legislatures to regulate interest rates more rigorously. Dr. Black is passionate about ensuring that people have access to valid and diverse sources of credit. Although it may seem counterintuitive, he's concerned about stringent government regulation of interest rates.

Debates about interest-rate regulation have been raging since the days of Aristotle. But why does this debate matter to us now? As it turns out, even with the best of intentions, such regulations could damage the very form of credit that, I was learning, encourages conscious borrowing. Dr. Black explained that such rules often mean that traditional consumer installment lenders simply can't afford to provide the relatively small amounts of money that their customers often need.

In our meeting at the University of Tennessee, Dr. Black observed, "People need money for legitimate reasons. And when people need it, they go to whatever source makes it available, regulated or otherwise. In places where the consumer installment loan industry has been overregulated to the point that it can no longer survive, the industry disappears. When these licensed sources dry up, people go to pawnbrokers, loan sharks, and other nonregulated loan sources. They rely more on expensive overdraft loans from their checking accounts. And when that happens, stress mounts. People become worse off financially. They incur higher debt burdens, which leads to greater strife within families, including more divorces. The ironic thing is that research shows that when excessive regulation is lifted and legitimate credit becomes available again, stress eases and people actually reduce their debt."

WHAT DO YOU OWE?

You've got to know what you owe. Write it down.
This small step can help you make better decisions.

Having a wealth of options is vitally important to creating a psychology of wealth—and to carrying out the practical work it takes to achieve prosperity. The time-tested installment loan seems to embody one of the remedies for what ails us financially, both individually and collectively. But might we be legislating this vital option out of existence? I found little evidence that most people—including legislators—understood what was happening or what we're in danger of losing. Clearly, more education is needed. Without responsible options that allow conscious borrowing, we may become more limited in our ability to move ahead financially, to achieve our goals, and to make smart bets on ourselves and our future.

And, as I was about to learn, the money lent and borrowed in this traditional way also has an energizing effect on communities.

RC Colas and MoonPies

I traveled to Nashville and introduced myself to Tennessee State Representative Johnny Shaw. When I walked into his office in the House of Representatives, he shook my hand and smiled the kind of smile that wrapped all the way to his sparkling eyes. We sat down to chat in front of a roaring fire. His posture was dignified, and his head was high. As a longtime professional broadcaster, he is poised and articulate. Now in his sixth term in the Tennessee legislature, he has owned a successful radio station for decades and has been pastor of the same church for more than 30 years. He is also the son of sharecroppers.

As a respected legislator, Representative Shaw has held a variety of official roles in his state.[7] "Since my second term, I have been a member of the House Finance, Ways & Means Committee. That put me in a position to work with people who have helped me understand how finance works." The day I met with Representative Shaw, the House had just started a new session. He was on a break, and I asked if he would share his story.

"I was born in Fayette County, Tennessee, in a little community called Laconia. There was a store and a cotton gin. Going into what we called 'town' on weekends to get an RC Cola and a MoonPie was one of the greatest gratifications I've ever had. Those are days I shall never forget." Remembering what many would consider a poor childhood, he chuckled and shook his head, obviously enjoying the memory. "My mom and dad were sharecroppers. We were raised up *very* poor. We didn't know we were poor, because at the time that's the way people lived. I was raised on a farm in the country and grew up with good morals. My parents taught us all very good morals—we had morals like you would not believe! As kids, there were certain things we did and did not do. Our parents were very strict with us, and I thank

God for that now. Long story short, that's why I'm where I am today.

"When I was about 18 years old, my dad exercised his right to vote. That's when he was notified we had to move; he could not vote and continue to live on that land. We were going to have to move to Tent City. You may have read about this place, in Fayette County. By the grace of God, a landlord met my dad on the street that weekend and offered us a place in Hardeman County. Well, my dad and my family escaped Tent City just like that."

Understanding "Tent City"—and this distinguished man's origins—requires a brief history lesson. In 1959 and 1960, in two counties in Tennessee, black sharecroppers who had registered to vote or had even attempted to register were threatened, thrown off their land, and blacklisted by merchants. The evicted families ended up in a tent encampment, where they lived on dirt floors and were barred from buying food and gas. Tent City became the home of black families who now had no land, no money, and no food—but who wanted to vote. Some people lived in the encampment for up to two years. Their cause drew national media coverage and attracted the attention of the Kennedy administration. It resulted in the first federal lawsuit brought under the Civil Rights Act.[8]

"Hardeman County was the next county over," Representative Shaw continued. "It is where I finished high school and where we live now, in Bolivar. I went to Memphis State for a while and I got married, but I dropped out of school because my dad had passed away, and I had to go back home to help my mom on the farm. Afterward, I worked in a public job, but before long, I was in the ministry. When I first started pastoring in my church, they sent me back to school at the American Baptist Theological Seminary, in Nashville. I thought I was going to school to learn to be a better pastor. But I found out that school doesn't teach you that. Life does."

As he was beginning to pastor and becoming a community activist, Johnny Shaw also had a desire to go into business. He explained, "I had done some part-time radio work while I was in high school, and it had left me with the determination to own a radio station. One day the company I had worked for approached me. They said, 'We've got a radio station we want to sell. Do you want to buy it?' Because of the installment loan company I had used before, I was able to gather the down payment. The loan came through, and I bought that radio station. Since then, I've been pretty successful."

I was surprised to learn that this remarkable man's life in business had started with a consumer installment loan. I had also begun to see a common thread in my conversations with Representative Shaw, Bennie Taylor, and many others who had used these loans: the sense of self-reliance that these loans had offered them.

AN IMPORTANT TIP

Make it a point to pay off one debt and then the next and the next. When you have paid one off, this will give you a sense of accomplishment and encourage you to tackle your next goal.

Representative Shaw supported the impression that I had gained in my research: "An installment loan program offers dignity in lending. I think that if you look at the whole pie—at the various financing options that are available to people—each option represents a slice of that pie. Different people need different slices. I think that's important for people like myself—like a schoolteacher, a local worker, or a family with several children.

"These kinds of options give you a chance to look forward to things that you thought you might never be able to do or to own. You're automatically building your future. You make an obligation that you have to meet. As you do, you can borrow more and you can continue to build on your future. That's what it's all about."

Representative Shaw continued, "Most successful people use borrowed finances to become successful. It gives us an opportunity to build our lives in a comfortable way and, at the same time, enjoy the necessities of life and some of the things we want as we go about creating our future."

Energizing the Community

Representative Shaw also observed yet a broader value of installment loans—namely, their value for towns and communities. He explained, "Local residents who come into a local installment loan office to borrow money spend that money in the community. Someone borrows for a refrigerator, someone else for an air conditioner or for school clothes for their kids. The money is spent right there. The local businesses use the money to pay their employees, and their employees shop within the community, too. As you circulate this money, you're building not only your own future, but your community's as well."

I do believe that it's possible to go from poverty even to wealth. It starts with knowing what you value and then being obedient to what you want to do.
—Representative Johnny Shaw

In parting, I asked this wise community servant for his insight about success. He replied, "You have to know what you value. To me, that means deciding that you can do what you want to do in life. You have to be determined. If you set your mind to it, and you really get out there and work at it, nobody can stop you.

"I do believe that it's possible to go from poverty even to wealth. It starts with knowing what you value and then being *obedient* to what you want to do. By that, I mean you must find what you value most and stick with it. Be devoted to that, and you'll learn as you go along. That's what I've done over the years. It's an education you get on the job, so to speak, and it's as valuable as any you can ever get. If you stick with what you value and follow your dreams, you too can learn from life. It's a great teacher."

Living Consciously

*Living in the moment means letting go of
the past and not waiting for the future. It
means living your life consciously, aware
that each moment you breathe is a gift.*

—Oprah Winfrey

Some people know J. C. Watts because he played football. He
was a high school athlete who became the star quarterback
for the University of Oklahoma, where he led his team to con-
secutive Orange Bowl victories. Other people remember that J.C.
had made history as one of the first two black students to attend
an integrated elementary school in Eufaula, Oklahoma, where
he grew up. Still others know him as a former member of the
U.S. Congress; after a successful professional football career, J.C.
served in the House of Representatives from 1995 to 2002. However one knows him, J. C. Watts is a remarkable man.

One of the most striking parts of his story is his decision to
take a political stand quite different from that of his family. Most
people in his impoverished rural neighborhood were Democrats,
and the people he held most dear were Democratic community
leaders and activists. J.C. was also an activist, but one with a
different point of view. "I was willing to step away, because I

wanted to examine issues that I felt were important from a new perspective."

When he entered his first political race in 1990, he took a chance on his independent views by entering as a Republican. With his victory, he became the first black candidate elected to statewide office in Oklahoma. Later, in the U.S. House, J.C. would win a Republican Party leadership position, becoming the first African American to do so in the history of the U.S. Congress.

"Individual greatness comes from accepting personal responsibility," is a view that J.C. and I share. His story embodies an important aspect of a psychology of wealth: we must be willing not only to accept responsibility but also to take a chance on ourselves in order to achieve our broader goals—particularly now. "This is no time to hide," J.C. says about the current economic crisis. "It is no time to hold back. It is time to invest in ourselves, to find a way to move forward, personally and as a nation. The whole world is facing a critical moment now. It is an important time, when we must have the courage to take some chances and to step up and seize opportunities wherever we may find them. If there is an ounce of potential within us that we can harvest, and we do not, we are selling ourselves short."

"I almost dropped out of college a couple of times," he recalls. "My father encouraged me to stay. It was tough. I got married when I was a freshman, in 1977. My wife and I had a child, and we were doing all we could to survive. Our parents weren't able to give us money every month. Also, understandably, they believed that we had made our bed, and so it was ours to lie in. We had next to nothing, and now I wonder how we made it, but we just did what we had to do. After we had our second child, we needed a new refrigerator. We discovered that when you have very little income, you stretch and sometimes you borrow. I went to an installment loan company and got what we needed to buy that refrigerator and keep the milk cold and the food fresh for our kids. It taught us responsibility, and I'm grateful for the experience. I was also thankful to have options."

"It was hard to keep stretching and moving ahead when each step felt like a burden. But hard times," he says, "are the ones in which we grow and learn. Everyone wants to move forward, to grow and change—people want to evolve. We shouldn't shut down as individuals or as a nation because times are hard. We have to prepare ourselves for the future, to create—and to protect—opportunities for people.

"Personal responsibility is often misinterpreted in politics. To me, it simply means that at some point I have to realize that I'm the common denominator in everything that happens to me. I must be responsible for both the good *and* the bad choices I make. The successful organizations I've been involved with—football teams, churches, businesses—know this. If we're not succeeding, we need to ask what we can do differently."

The conversation with J.C. caused me to think about opportunity and risk, and their role in a healthy wealth psychology. Next, it was time to meet Dr. Frederick Miller.

Then and Now

Dr. Miller was in the process of retiring from the University of Oklahoma when I first met him. He sat in his office, surrounded by the fruits of his labors in the fields of commercial and consumer law. The stacks of publications and manuscripts documented his work and that of other great minds of the nation. Compared to his accomplishments, Dr. Miller is modest. He's a little stiff after years of fine dining and travel, and he's hoping to get his knees working better, but his mind is razor-sharp.

I was becoming increasingly curious about how social and cultural changes are affecting our individual relationships with money and prosperity. Today we are slowly recovering from what is already being called the Great Recession. In one way or another, this economic earthquake has touched the lives of virtually everyone. It has made many of us reexamine our approach to spending, borrowing, risk, and living in general. Many of us also wonder how we've come to this not-so-pretty pass. I wanted to hear Dr. Miller's perspective on that very question, particularly on the social impact of how money is borrowed and loaned. He had some history to share. I was reminded that there was a time when people's financial options were so limited that, although it may have been difficult to overborrow and overspend, it was also very tough to get ahead.

"In the past, credit was available only to a certain class," he began. "The result was that some people were able to have a very nice lifestyle. Others, who couldn't obtain credit, had a hard time bettering themselves." Those who were not wealthy had few, if any, options for borrowing money. Although many ordinary folks could use consumer installment loans to buy specific goods, only the wealthy could readily borrow cash. This created a critical divide. The inability to borrow money severely limited an individual's options, both for meeting basic needs and for making investments in the future.

"The credit market was effectively segregated by law," Dr. Miller continued. "That is to say, there were usury statutes— determinations by legislatures that you couldn't pay more than a certain amount for interest. But there were a lot of exceptions— for example, for banks. So, if you were the kind of customer that a bank would be interested in, you might be able to get credit despite these caps. The Small Loan Acts, laws first enacted in the

1920s, were designed to allow people other than those favored by banks to borrow cash. The trade-off was a high degree of regulation."

As we talked, Dr. Miller confirmed what I had learned about the overall growth of prosperity—namely, that credit was a stimulus for the expansion of a strong and flourishing middle class. Access to credit also helped to shrink the great economic class divide. But has our individual and collective relationship with money and credit become so fraught and anxious that the power of credit to improve our lives has been eliminated?

The Dream of Prosperity

As we work to climb out of the recession, many people are still feeling the effects of job losses, defaults on mortgages, and a volatile stock market. With the global economic crisis of 2008, the dream of middle-class prosperity took a serious blow. And, as discussed in the last chapter, credit played a central role. "America's middle class is hurting," said U.S. Vice President Joe Biden in January of 2009. "It is our charge to get the middle class— the backbone of this country—up and running again." As writer Claire Suddath quipped in *Time*, "One could practically hear the cheers emanating from single-family homes with two-car garages."[1]

We're all familiar with the spate of runaway spending and borrowing that preceded the crisis. Many Americans and their neighbors around the world were buying things that they couldn't afford—most notably, houses—at breathtaking rates. The role that subprime mortgages played in the painful reckoning of our economy is well known. With the complicity of banks, average citizens were piling up mountains of debt that they couldn't necessarily support. As of early 2009, "About 21% of middle-class Americans had spent themselves to the limit. Personal bankruptcies rose by a third from [2008], and mortgage defaults—well, they're moving beyond subprime borrowers and hitting those with previously high credit scores."[2]

During the spree, few people wanted to talk about the consequences of this reckless borrowing and consumption. In retrospect, we wonder: how could we have accumulated these unsupportable levels of debt—both individually and collectively—when history has shown us that such extremes lead to spectacular economic crashes?

RECOGNIZING AND CONTROLLING UNCONSCIOUS DEBT

Five Signs of Unconscious Debt

- You find items that you forgot you had purchased on credit and that you have never used or worn.

- You have a TV/DVD/CD player in every room, but you have trouble paying your bills.

- You are purchasing things with credit without knowing how much you are paying.

- Your credit cards are maxed out, and you can't remember what you bought.

- You are still making payments on things you no longer own.

Three Steps to Help You Control
Unconscious Debt

- Ask yourself, "Do I *want* or do I *need* this item?" If it is only a want, does it fit your budget?

- Avoid binge shopping. Put the item on hold; if you forget about it, you don't need it.

- Make a plan for goals you'd like to work toward. Discuss your plan with a spouse, partner, or friend.

May I Borrow a Cup of Sugar?

Throughout history, in all places and at all times, credit has eased and facilitated social life. Prosperity and credit go hand in hand. Most of us couldn't get through a day without some form of lending and borrowing. Can I lend a hand? May I borrow a cup of sugar? An umbrella? A pen? A moment of your time? These exchanges require trust and imply an interdependence that society simply could not function without. Receiving and bestowing credit are deeply human and social activities, and they are certainly essential tools for creating prosperity.

As I had learned, credit played a key role in the meteoric rise of the U.S. economy during the Industrial Revolution and afterward. In the 1800s, the ability of people with moderate incomes to borrow fueled the emergence of a thriving middle class. Today, in many places around the world, microlending is helping to open economic doors for people who want a better life.

Early installment credit plans paved and widened the path to advancement for middle-income Americans. Similar plans followed rapidly, allowing millions of average citizens to buy cars and other items that had previously been out of their reach. This purchasing power not only provided a way to improve the quality of life, but also freed many people to pursue dreams of greater achievement while, at the same time, opening the door to greater wealth and prosperity in America and around the world.

Checking the Rearview Mirror

By the turn of the twenty-first century, however, something was seriously amiss in the use of credit. Many factors contributed to the rise of debt and the fall of the economy near the end of this century's first decade. But among them was a culture that seemed to be giving us carte blanche permission—and even encouragement—to spend well beyond our means. We borrowed and bought without looking either in the rearview mirror or at the road ahead. Behind us, a mountain of debt was accumulating, and there had been so many job losses that the means of paying it off was threatened. Many people had lapsed into unconscious habits of consumption and debt. For some, the imperative was to live well, but not to think about the consequences or the bill that would come due sooner or later.

I vividly recall an intelligent and sophisticated friend remarking to me in 2000, "Everyone I know is up to their eyeballs in debt. That's just what you do now." She was explaining why she simply wasn't going to worry about having tapped out her home equity line and accepted every credit card offer that arrived in the mail. It was easy for otherwise smart people to get swept up in the tide of good times that seemed to be available simply by virtue of being a consumer.

But even then, cracks were beginning to show. Driving down a typical suburban street, one could observe the facades of large

IDENTIFYING CONSCIOUS DEBT

Conscious Debt

1. Allows you to move forward in life.

2. Has a specific repayment plan and fixed payment amounts.

3. Is based on what your income is now, not on what it might be.

4. Does not come from impulse buying.

5. Is paid off before the goods or services are used up.

6. Improves the quality of your life without sacrificing basic necessities.

7. Helps you manage your finances.

8. Is part of a planned financial budget.

9. Makes you feel good for longer than it takes to make the purchase.

and apparently prosperous homes. However, inside many of these homes, a real estate agent confessed to me, were barren rooms with little furniture. The owners had maxed out their resources with the purchase of the house and were running on financial fumes. When many of his clients bought their homes, the agent continued, they had assumed that funds would somehow continue to be available indefinitely. Repayment would come sometime far in the future, if ever.

We had closed our eyes to the consequences of how we were borrowing, using, and relating to our money. Things were clearly out of balance. Credit was the fuel of our advancement, but it appeared that we, as a culture, had stopped using debt consciously and judiciously. Not everyone fell prey to this lack of discrimination, of course. But enough did that the aggregate results of this unconsciously acquired debt were catastrophic—both for millions of individuals and for our economy as a whole.

The Pendulum Does Its Thing

I have observed in my friends, associates, clients, and the world at large an interesting fact about human nature: when we make a mistake, a natural desire to correct our course can cause an overreaction that moves us too far in the opposite direction. It's pretty basic psychology. As with a fishtailing car, as we try to compensate for our error, we can go right off the road. It appears that this natural tendency to overcompensate may be at play in our cultural attitudes toward money.

Because the economic crisis resulted in part from unconscious spending and lending, the cultural pendulum has swung the other way. From a certain acceptance of extravagant purchasing and borrowing—and subtle and not-so-subtle encouragement to ignore the consequences—the popular wisdom has become: "Hunker down and don't spend a penny more than is absolutely necessary. We have to play it safe. The future is uncertain. Better to save and lie low until the economic picture improves. Debt is to be avoided at all costs. Circle the wagons, and take no risks."

As with a fishtailing car, as we try to compensate for our error, we can go right off the road.

Some popular financial advisors deliver strict and persuasive warnings about the use of credit, and they counsel us accordingly. Before we make any expenditure, they exhort us to ask ourselves: "Do I need it, or do I want it?" The assumption is that "needs" encompass life's most elemental requirements (such as food, basic shelter, clothing, and transportation), and also savings and retirement plans. All other expenditures are to be considered suspect and denied as self-indulgent *wants*. *Loan* and *debt* have become four-letter words.

Some advisors also encourage us to reclaim the idealized values and practices of earlier times. But, most likely, such times never existed. As a recent Harvard Business School publication observed, "There is a myth of a lost golden age of economic virtue. Once upon a time, the story goes, people lived within their means and borrowed only under the direst of circumstances. Debt was shameful, and credit financed only 'productive' purchases like homes or farm machinery. Although nostalgia seldom makes good history, writers mourned this lost golden age during the Roaring Twenties, the rise of the credit card in the 1960s, and the home mortgage boom and bust of 2005–2008. . . . [Yet] credit itself is as old as commerce."[3]

Nonetheless, some of the popular financial advice has gold at its core. To stop and consider our purchases and our borrowing before we take a plunge is wise. This is conscious financial decision making. Any change that requires us to become more conscious of our behavior is a welcome and necessary course correction. Indeed, it was the general heedlessness with which many people jumped into financial deep water that, in part, got the United States and others nations into trouble.

But has the pendulum swung too far the other way? In our attempt to repair the damage done by unconscious spending and borrowing, are we taking the belt-tightening and self-denial too far for our own good?

Bob Muster is a dentist whose experience reveals one way this issue comes up in our daily lives—that is, in our teeth. In a July 2011 article in the *Dayton Daily News*, Muster said he understands "that money is tight for many families, but preventive care makes more financial sense in the long run." He explained, "I consider getting your teeth cleaned every six months like getting oil changes for your car—it keeps your engine from blowing up. It's much less expensive to do preventive maintenance than a complete overhaul." In the same article, Dr. Michael Dickerson of Troy, Ohio, explained how "a little financial planning can help people avoid higher costs down the road and life-long problems."[4] Tightening the belt too severely can become more expensive in the long run. We cannot create balance by swinging so far to the other side that we run right off the road. Overcompensation does not create balance.

Creating a robust psychology of wealth requires a healthy balance of saving and investing in oneself.

Today many people fear that they don't have enough money or that they won't have enough to carry them through an uncertain future. Fear in itself is constrictive and disempowering. It can feed on itself, and it rarely leads to balanced and constructive decisions. The famous misers of the nineteenth century, Hetty Green and Russell Sage, are the not-so-shining examples of the extremes that the fear of loss and want can lead to. (In the next chapter, you'll learn more about the lengths to which these curious characters took frugality.) Allowing fear to keep us from spending money is certainly counterproductive for creating prosperity.

Common sense tells us that saving and setting aside money for emergencies is a prudent practice. The sense of security that savings can bring is worth its weight in gold. For building a wealth-enhancing sense of self-esteem, saving money certainly does no harm. However, creating a robust psychology of wealth requires a healthy balance of saving and investing in oneself. Creating a financial cushion is beneficial. But it simply doesn't have the same potent impact on self-esteem—or the potential to create prosperity—that growing, expanding, and taking action can.

From the false-bottomed boom preceding the big bust, we learned that having a glut of possessions, gadgets, and vehicles isn't the same as being prosperous. Nor, of course, is having a burdensome level of debt. Yet extreme self-restriction and a fearful elimination of all risk taking can severely limit our ability to move forward in life. Not only will financial austerity and avoidance of all investment and debt keep us stuck in our individual lives, but it could have a negative effect on the economy at large. The responsible flow of credit—and the social trust that it requires and engenders—is essential to the commerce of life. Neither of the extremes—heedlessness or inflexible financial abstinence—is likely to lead to prosperity.

A New Perspective

So what will get us out of the unfortunate spot we've gotten ourselves into? In a word: consciousness.

Approaching our finances consciously—with an awareness of our circumstances, motivations, and true aims—is a key. With this kind of consciousness, we assess what is meaningful to us and what we must do in order to bring that meaning to fruition. We also acknowledge that we may need to take risks in order to move forward. We take realistic stock of what a particular risk involves and of our ability to take that risk without damaging ourselves or others. And then, if we decide that it's in our best interest to do so, we bet on ourselves. And if we want to borrow money, we do so knowing how and when we will pay it back.

When is stretching or taking a risk a reasonable and conscious act? Was Representative Johnny Shaw's ambitious decision to buy a radio station reasonable and responsible? Bennie Taylor made a choice when he borrowed funds for a trip to commemorate his grandfather. Senator Leticia Van de Putte's family made similar choices when they made investments in their business to give their family a shot at a good life.

None of these investments were impulsive, perilous, or burdensome. The risks that these thoughtful and optimistic people took were not to satisfy what might appear to be simple "wants." These were conscious investments in their own futures and in lives that were meaningful to them. Perhaps most telling, all these people made choices to keep up with no one but an inner voice that told them they were worth the stretch.

Money Matters

Jeff Burch teaches U.S. military personnel how to make conscious decisions about money. For the past 20 years, he has been assisting active-duty service members in learning how to manage their finances in the unique circumstances of military life.

Jeff explains, "Military personnel are required to be alert and ready for service. Financial preparedness and being ready for duty go hand in hand." Being financially prepared in any walk of life means being careful with your money—saving, building good credit, and using debt wisely. "But it's particularly important in the military," Jeff says, "because service members live under a mandate to keep their finances in order. Otherwise they can be dishonorably discharged. The reason is straightforward: carrying too much debt creates stress, and stress is a distraction. A service member whose mind is on other things can't focus on the job. It may sound like a simple thing, but having a balanced budget and solid credit are important aspects of each member's military readiness. When the people who serve are on solid financial footing, it helps the nation's military stay focused and strong."[5]

Balance, responsibility, and discipline: these are all good guideposts for achieving prosperity in any walk of life.

He observes, "Contrary to a common perception, military personnel overall have a higher level of education and financial literacy than the general public. Their responsibility level is high, too. They're ready to put their lives on the line on short notice, so every aspect of their lives needs to be as balanced as possible. Their relationship with money has to be disciplined. Discipline is paying attention and practicing restraint. In this case, it means paying attention to how they use their money."

Balance, responsibility, and discipline: these are all good guideposts for achieving prosperity in any walk of life. Jeff expands on the idea of balance from a military perspective: "In the service, the men and women are prepared, but they don't live in fear. When it comes to finances, I counsel that no one should spend blindly or recklessly, with no thought of the future. But it's healthy to leave some room for the occasional frivolous purchase, if you can. Squeezing down too tightly can feel like we are not living."

He concludes, "Like military preparedness, financial preparedness is an attitude of calm alertness. That state of mind and approach to money creates a life with more ease, less stress, and readiness for whatever comes next."

With military precision, Jeff had just described a healthy relationship with money.

A Very Conscious Decision

Dr. Miller, the consumer law expert, knows the value of a dollar, so I asked him about the ways he believes he has made healthy investments in his own life. In response, he told a story of summer vacations and family.

"I belong to an organization that holds an annual meeting in the summer," he replied, "where we sit around and discuss law. I think my life would have been much less rich without those gatherings. One of the reasons I feel that way is that I always made sure my wife and my two sons came with me. If you're going to be gone for more than a week and you don't bring your wife and children with you, you're deprived of their company and of a lot of memorable experiences."

He laughed as he moved to the next part of the story. More than once, he didn't have the money to pay for these adventures. "At that time, since I was a poor law professor, we didn't have the money to pay for these trips out of savings. So what we'd do, in effect, is finance them with a credit card. We knew we could pay it off, because we usually were reimbursed. The cost of the short-term debt was well worth it. It was important to me that my family came along."

When I met Marcia, Dr. Miller's wife of 52 years, she admitted that borrowing the money was a big deal to her husband. It was obviously a very conscious decision. "Fred is *very* thrifty, very careful," she explained. "He always reads the fine print. It's part of his heritage. After the Great Depression, his grandfather lost a great deal of money and became very frugal. Unbeknownst to the family, he kept his cash in the books in his office. When he passed away, the family discovered it. The money came falling out of the books as they were being packed off for donations. At the time, it was a lot of money." Fred doesn't hide his money in books, but, "He's someone who drives the same car for 15 years," Marcia laughed. "Fred doesn't do anything without conscious consideration."

So what about those vacations on credit? He explained, "Well, borrowing for that kind of experience, it seems to me, is an example of borrowing with a real benefit. It made a big difference to me and to my family. The kids made a lot of friends from all over the country and got to see a lot of places. And, of course, they had the companionship they would have lost had they not been with us during that time. To me, it was well worth it." Marcia agreed. "Those trips were wonderful. We still have great friends from those meetings." And, she added, "Fred also knew we could pay back the loans."

Like many Americans and people around the world, the Millers stretched themselves to make life better for their children—and for the Millers' goals, this required a big stretch. "To keep the kids in college," Marcia related, "we got a home equity line of credit—after we had paid off the house. It took 20 years to get both boys out of college, with two degrees each. We told them it was like baseball—three and you're out! It was expensive, but it was worth it. I taught school, and Fred worked seven days a week, and the boys had some other help. Somehow we got through it. In fact, I thought this was going to be a way of life, and we would never get them out of school," she confessed with a hint of humor, "but we're glad we did it. We helped them get out of college debt-free. We're happy about what they have achieved; both are doing well. It was a good investment."

What struck me most was the Millers' determination to catapult their sons ahead in life while keeping their eyes wide open to what that would mean in terms of hard work. You don't have to be afraid to take a risk. You just have to be prepared to do the work.

You don't have to be afraid to take a risk. You just have to be prepared to do the work.

Soon after our conversation, Dr. Miller and Marcia moved to Minnesota to be close to their family, and I visited him there as well. Their home is comfortable and beautiful, filled with souvenirs from their travels all over the world. I asked him about his views on wealth and its meaning. "I think it's important to have the perspective that wealth is not measured just by what you have. It shouldn't be measured by whether you have a Cadillac or a Chevy, whether you have a mansion or an apartment. It's ultimately more of an intangible thing. It's about having freedom and the ability to do things you can't otherwise do."

We talked about the American Dream, which may be suffering a little of late, but the spirit of which is still felt by everyone who wants to get ahead and achieve a measure of prosperity. "I think the American Dream embodies our hopes to step up on our own merits."

Dr. Miller feels that prosperity "is a mark of your success, which often reflects your sense of self-worth." He said the reward is "the confidence that your success gives you and the sense that you've made a contribution to society."

Moving Forward

It is human nature to want to expand, grow, explore, and stretch boundaries. It is what brought people to the New World, and it continues to inspire dreams of prosperity all over the world. To limit or dampen that abiding and generous drive is certainly not desirable.

Today we have many options for ways to give ourselves a hand up in life and to achieve prosperity for ourselves and our loved ones. These include both monetary and nonmonetary options. But the specific ways in which we invest in our prosperity matter far less than the awareness and value the experience provides. To achieve real prosperity requires us to buy, borrow, invest, and, most important, live consciously. Money that is used consciously can move us ahead without endangering our individual or collective welfare. It can empower, invigorate, and fuel our growth. This perspective holds great promise for a new psychology of wealth.

The Power of Giving Back

We make a living by what we get. We make a life by what we give.

—Winston Churchill

In 2005, Lee had the opportunity to serve a nonprofit organization for one year. For as many years as I had known him, he had made it a habit to give to this organization in any way he could. Generally his contribution was in the form of financial donations and several commitments each year to volunteer at events. This new project, however, was something special and would be demanding. Accepting the offer would mean a great deal of travel, as well as reduced time with his family and a considerable loss of income, since his own public relations company would have to take a backseat to this volunteer project with the nonprofit. Yet he believed in the organization and wanted to invest his time and energy to help it achieve specific goals. Lee and his wife discussed the idea carefully and decided that he should accept the proposal. Lee's wife would work harder to make up for his absence at home as much as possible, and later they would both try to make up for the loss of income and get their finances back on track. They would be apart quite a bit, and it would certainly be a big sacrifice from a financial perspective, but they both felt good about making the pledge and the agreement.

Lee began the project excitedly, but during the first few months away from home, he grew weary. The project's demands were many. On one long, late plane ride home, he found himself questioning the wisdom of his decision. After several hours of mulling, he decided that his belief in the principle of service was most important. Ultimately he saw his work on the project as an opportunity to give back, and he knew that he was in a unique position to provide what was needed. He recommitted to the project in his heart and resolved not to question his decision again.

In the fourth month, Lee was in Seattle waiting for a delayed flight when he received a call from a business client that he had worked with for the last 10 years. The client wanted him to come in to discuss a major project that it hoped to start right away. Lee hardly knew how he could turn down the handsome financial offer he was sure would be involved. But he had made a commitment to the nonprofit, and he intended to stand by it, even if it would hurt his own company's earnings. He explained to the client that he was already committed to another project, but he agreed, as a courtesy, to go in for a visit while he was home. His intention was to turn down the offer, but he would at least keep the door open for future work.

When Lee arrived at the client's office and sat down to talk with the company vice president, the man quietly slid a check across the table to Lee. Looking at the dollar amount of the check, Lee smiled somewhat sadly and reminded the executive of the nonprofit project he was working on. "I really wish I could accept this," he admitted, "and it is a generous offer, but I am completely committed for at least a year, maybe a little more. If your project will wait, I would love to do it, but I understand if you need to move forward without me."

"We don't mind if you're busy," replied the executive. "Fit the project in whenever you can. We'd rather have you busy than not have you at all." Lee shook his head and said plainly that he wished he were able to accept the job, but he simply couldn't. He pushed the check back across the desk. The vice president surprised him by shaking his head and refusing to take back the check. "Just keep the money. Cash the check." The executive smiled and nodded as if everything were settled.

Lee was stumped. He felt that he couldn't possibly do the work that was being offered while he was busy traveling. He didn't wish to compromise his current commitment. On the other hand, he didn't want to disappoint his business client. How could he possibly accept the money?

The conversation with the executive went back and forth for several minutes, with Lee suggesting that the company find someone else to do the job and the executive insisting that Lee keep the check and do some work whenever he had a little extra time— no pressure, no need to compromise his existing commitments. "Take all the time you need," the executive repeated. Finally, Lee asked sincerely, "But what if I can't do what you're asking? What if it's too overwhelming with what I am already doing?"

The man replied, "We'd rather have you take the money, and we trust that if it's right, you'll find a way. If you fail, just keep the money! We don't want you to compromise what you are doing, but we'd rather give you the project than give it to someone else. The project is yours, whether or not you can do it now." He stood up to walk out of the office with Lee.

Lee was now curious. "Why are you so insistent that I do the work?" he asked. The executive explained, "Six years ago we had a conversation in which you made a recommendation that would help move our company forward. This was your idea, Lee. We've been very slow to pick up on it, but we're ready now. And since it was your idea, you are the only person we are interested in having do the work." Lee's memory returned slowly to the original conversation. He had forgotten about his suggestion long ago. As they walked out together, Lee looked at the check again. He noticed that the amount was exactly what he had given up so far by doing the volunteer work. He also realized that if he got the client's assignment done, he would have yet another check coming at the end of the project, totaling much more than he would have made during a normal year.

Lee discussed the situation with his wife and with the director of the nonprofit. They all agreed that there was no conflict. Everyone was happy. All Lee would have to do for his client was to make phone calls between presentations and meetings for the nonprofit. With his wife's and the nonprofit director's encouragement and support, Lee agreed to take on the new work. He left on his flight the next day with a light heart.

His work for the nonprofit was far more successful than anyone had anticipated. His travels extended for many extra months—taking him as far as Alaska, Europe, and Australia—and involved more time than had originally been agreed upon. But during that time, Lee managed to complete the business project, and, as promised, a large commission check awaited him when he returned home late one night. His wife had put the check on his desk with a note that said, "Good work!" Under the check was a stack of thank-you cards from people he had met during his recent travels—heartfelt messages of appreciation and gratitude. But Lee felt that he was the most grateful. To him, it seemed astounding that life could work out with such balance and grace. He had heard a saying once: "You can't out-give God." To him it meant that whatever you give with an open heart will naturally come back to you—not because you expect it, but because you don't.

The Power of Giving

One of the joys of experiencing prosperity is having the ability to give back—to take care of ourselves so well that we can afford to share with others abundantly. This giving can take many forms, from helping a friend in a time of need to making a donation to a beloved alma mater, contributing to health-care research, volunteering with the Scouts, or supporting a church or some other nonprofit organization. Giving raises our self-esteem and our sense of responsibility to ourselves and others. It is a fascinating aspect of the psychology of wealth that in giving to others, we often open the door wider for our own prosperity. Generosity also offers the opportunity to experience wealth of the greatest kind—a life of richness and fulfillment. The returns in terms of our personal growth from selfless giving cannot be overestimated. The more we give, the more we grow. As we progress, our capacity to receive and give back should do likewise—one feeds the other and generates the momentum needed to create a life of prosperity.

FUNNY HOW THAT WORKS

When you are feeling down, do something kind for someone else. A kindness given is also a gift to yourself.

When we hear the term *giving* associated with money, we often think of charitable giving or philanthropy. To be sure, this is an essential type of financial altruism. It can exemplify acts of selfless generosity, since the giver usually expects and receives no material benefit in return. Among its many gifts to individuals and society, philanthropy has underwritten the education of millions and saved many more from disease and natural disasters. Yet generosity can encompass any type of giving: that of one's time, talents, or money. It is the open heart and generous spirit with which we give that matters. With this spirit, we add both to the lives of others and to our own.

The truly wealthy give to others on a regular basis. Successful societies, nations, companies, and individuals understand the inherent benefits of generosity. Social and business leaders realize the value and significance of giving back in some form; this explains why they contribute to charities and other nonprofit organizations regularly.

Russell and Hetty

In many aspects of the psychology of wealth, we can sometimes learn much from observing people who have *not* adopted this psychology. In the late nineteenth century, Russell Sage amassed a fortune as a financier and railroad executive. Known for being extraordinarily tight with his money, he was convicted and fined for running a scheme that charged exorbitant interest for loans. In 1891, he was the victim of a failed assassination attempt. Afterward, his clerk, William Laidlaw, accused Sage of having used him as a human shield. The clerk was disabled for life, but Sage fought attempts to compensate him. His clerk won two lawsuits at trial; however, despite the judgments against the wealthy Sage, the clerk never received a cent and was forced to depend on others for his support. Sage left all his money to his second wife and would probably have turned over in his grave if he had known how his vast fortune was eventually spent. She used a major portion of Sage's $70 million bequest for philanthropy, including funding the Russell Sage Foundation.

Hetty Green also left a legacy of vast wealth along with a portrait of miserly unhappiness. The first American woman to play a substantial role on Wall Street, she was also famous for her outlandish stinginess. "Green was that rarity: a woman who largely through her own efforts amassed a ton of money during the Gilded Age, a time when virtually everyone else getting rich—Rockefeller, Morgan, Carnegie—was a man. By nearly all accounts she was also a thoroughly unpleasant individual, greedy, petty and often downright nasty."[1]

Green was raised as a strict Quaker by a father who took the religion's tenets of humility and self-denial to extremes, while disregarding its doctrine of charity. Hetty's father praised her when she dressed in dirty rags, and she seemed to take pride in her austerity. As a staggeringly wealthy adult, she built a fortune but spent as little as possible, living with relatives to avoid having to pay rent and taxes. She wore old clothes and tried to resell the morning paper after she had read it. Clearly, the austerity programming that she received from her father was never modified!

When she heard that her Aunt Sylvia had willed $2 million to charity, Green challenged the will's validity in court by producing an earlier document claiming that her aunt had left her entire estate to Green. The case was ultimately decided against Green with a ruling that the document had been forged. Sadly, Green did not properly care for her 14-year-old son when he dislocated his kneecap in a sledding accident. She considered the doctor's fee too high, so she pretended to be a pauper in order to have him treated as a charity patient. When she was recognized at the free clinic, she left in a huff and tried to treat him herself. Her delay later cost him his leg.

Green's extreme attachment to her money ruined not only her reputation, but her life. She took no pleasure in her fortune. She left her genial husband because he had made bad investments. She trusted no one and lived in constant fear of assassination by relatives who would inherit when she died. Today, Hetty Green might be considered mentally ill and an obsessive-compulsive hoarder. (In her day, the rich were considered eccentric when others were called mad.) Nonetheless, she remains a classic example of the principle that when we do not give to others—or to ourselves—life becomes a wasted treasure.

It offends our sense of justice that Scrooges like Sage and Green can create financial abundance. It seems contrary to our instincts and to nature itself when people with tremendous financial resources are stingy or miserly. But, of course, it happens frequently. Generosity of spirit is not required in order to make a lot of money. But do these folks possess true wealth? Not likely. Are they respected and treasured, with a loving and supportive circle of friends, family, and associates? Without those resources, their stories become classic tales of having all the money in the world and no sense of joy—and no true prosperity. This is the shadow side of wealth. Living in fear and insecurity or with anger and resentment, these individuals become so absorbed with holding on to what they have that they miss out on the real riches of life.

No one can become rich without enriching others.
Anyone who adds to prosperity must prosper in turn.

—G. Alexander Orndorff

The Virtuous Circle

Our instincts also tell us that generosity is necessary to create a good life—one with balance, happiness, and a satisfying level of financial prosperity. Giving is both personally fulfilling and wealth-enhancing. It encourages the fullest possible flow of life and prosperity. A full container can hold more only when some of its volume is released.

The adage, "As you give, so shall you receive," defines a fundamental aspect of the psychology of wealth. The ways in which we give to others will come back to us many times over, and often in kind. If we give more love, more love will flow into our lives. If we give more freely of our finances, more financial opportunities may open for us. In short, when we give to others, we will feel the abundance in our own lives. This feeling enhances our sense of self-worth and, with it, our ability to reach our goals.

Taking on challenging tasks is a powerful way to build self-esteem. So is producing something that requires creativity or is nurturing to others. This nurturance is where giving comes in. When we help others solve a problem or improve their situation, we increase our own self-worth and expand the circle of prosperity. We create a virtuous circle in which everyone in our community, local and global, is uplifted.

Recently, when a friend of mine was in a doctor's waiting room, she overheard a conversation between the officer manager and a family regarding a bill that the family's insurance company had refused to pay. The mother of the family obviously needed care, but the manager told her that the $200 bill must be paid before she could receive additional services from the doctor. The discussion was calm, but the family was clearly strained by the news. With an air of resignation and a promise to return with their checkbook, the family started to leave the office. My friend's heart opened, and she wondered whether she should help. She could afford it. As she reached for her purse, another woman in the waiting room stood up and walked outside with the family.

Several minutes later, the family and the woman returned together. The woman walked to the desk, pulled out two $100 bills, and paid the amount owed. The office manager smiled brilliantly in acknowledgment. The family was obviously touched and grateful, and the mother asked how they could express their thanks. The woman who had given so freely said that no thanks were needed and that no repayment would be accepted. She asked only that they help someone else when they themselves saw a need. "The room was filled with a visceral energy of joy—as if the heavens had opened and bestowed gifts on everyone in that room. It was tangible," my friend told me of the experience. "Everyone smiled and seemed more relaxed. Love filled the room, and we all felt it."

Herr Rosenau

When we make an effort to serve others in some manner, we often discover that success in some form is never far behind. Giving and service do not require wealth, but they do engender wealth of all kinds. In 1917, Alex Lurye, a Jewish American soldier from Duluth, Minnesota, found himself in a small German town called Seldes. It was a Friday night in 1917, near the end of World War I. Feeling lonely and out of place, he decided to see what the local Jewish population was like, and he entered the village synagogue. The Americans and the Germans had fought bitterly, and Lurye felt awkward standing among people who were nominally his enemies. He was soon greeted by a man named Herr Rosenau, who quickly made him feel at home. After the services, Herr Rosenau invited the serviceman to his house for the traditional Friday night meal. The beauty of a Sabbath dinner, together with the warmth and kindness of this German family, made a deep impression on the young man. Herr Rosenau and his family made Alex Lurye feel that he was not alone, and certainly not an enemy, although he was so far from home.

Lurye was not able to visit this good-hearted family again before the end of the war. When he finally returned to Duluth, he wrote a letter of thanks to Herr Rosenau, who had touched his life with such kindness. For reasons unknown, Herr Rosenau didn't answer the letter. Instead, he placed it in a desk drawer, where it rested for the next 21 years.

The habit of giving only enhances the desire to give.

—Walt Whitman

In the meantime, the Rosenaus' daughter had grown up and married a man named Eugen Wienberg. By 1938, the couple had three children. It was a bad time for German Jews. Now a grandfather, Herr Rosenau was disturbed by the dark future he saw for his family and his fellow Jews in Germany. One day, his 11-year-old grandson, Sigbert, was rummaging through Herr Rosenau's desk looking for something of interest, and a foreign postage stamp caught his eye. He pulled out the envelope with the American stamp. "Grandfather, may I have this?" he asked. With his grandfather's assent, the boy took the envelope home to his mother, who eyed it with curiosity. When she read the long-forgotten thank-you letter from the American serviceman, she had an idea. She and her husband had been looking for a way to leave an increasingly dangerous Germany. On a long shot, she decided to write Alex Lurye and ask if he would sponsor her family for possible immigration to America. One major obstacle was already evident: the envelope had no return address. She wrote her letter addressed simply to "Alex Lurye, Duluth, Minnesota."

In the two decades while Herr Rosenau's family had been growing up, Alex Lurye had become a wealthy businessman and was well known in the sizable city of Duluth. And so the postmaster easily found him and delivered the letter. Lurye replied immediately, pledging to help bring the Wienberg family to Minnesota. He kept his promise. The entire Wienberg family arrived in the United States in May of 1938. The Rosenaus followed soon after. In Duluth, the Wienbergs had to work hard to gain a foothold in their new country, sometimes taking two jobs each just to make it through the week. Despite the hard work, they were grateful to have escaped Germany and the destruction that soon befell German Jewry. Because of Herr Rosenau's simple act of kindness, with no thought of personal gain, their lives had been saved. In America, his family thrived and grew, as children, grandchildren, and now great-grandchildren came along. One man's generosity to a stranger had been repaid many times over with an infinitely precious gift.[2]

Getting the Flow Going

As a psychotherapist and an executive trainer, I've observed that for many people, the challenge is not finding ways to give but feeling comfortable with receiving. Most of us want to help others and believe in the value of providing a helping hand. Indeed, many people find it easier to give than to receive. However, if you are hesitant to receive from others, you impede the flow of abundance just as much as you do if you are hesitant to give. We can acquire only the level of prosperity that we are open and willing to receive. Both giving and receiving are an important part of a balanced and prosperous life.

Sometimes people hesitate to give because they are afraid that later they will not have enough. This feeling, however factually based it may seem, can be a self-fulfilling prophecy and is certainly self-defeating. We can regard money as a form of energy—energy that flows through our society, our economy, and our individual lives. We receive money in exchange for something that we give, usually our work, services, or ideas, and we give it in kind. In itself, money is neutral. As a form of energy, it is never truly lost.

The psychology of wealth requires trusting that, no matter what happens, we will have enough.

The psychology of wealth requires trusting that, no matter what happens, we will have enough. My friend Deidra recalls the time she learned this lesson in a powerful way. Deidra had a new teaching position in Cincinnati, Ohio. One day, after feeding coins into the machines at a Laundromat to wash her clothes, she was down to her last five dollars until her next paycheck. While she stood folding her laundry, a young man approached her selling raffle tickets for a charity called "The Neediest Kids of All." Just the name brought tears to her eyes. But the tickets cost five dollars. Deidra stood for a moment, considering. She had enough food and gas to get by, so she figured she'd be okay. She bought the last ticket the fellow had.

When she received a call saying that she had won the raffle, she didn't even know what the prize was. She hadn't asked! She had recently confessed to her students that she would love to go on a hot-air balloon ride, but it was beyond her budget. She had imagined how exciting it would be to float above the Ohio River, watching the brilliant colors of the autumn leaves. She had even called around in hopes of finding an affordable deal, but the fees had all exceeded her means. Sure enough, the prize she won that day was a hot-air balloon ride over the river, complete with press coverage, champagne, and a souvenir photo. Soon thereafter she was sailing over the fall terrain on a bright sunny day—and it was even better than she had imagined. The cost of that experience? One open heart, a willingness to give to others, and her last five-dollar bill. Deidra trusted that she would be okay and would have enough. With a healthy sense of self-esteem, she also trusted in her ability to create prosperity for herself.

Investing in Ourselves and Others

I often think of the biblical story in which a servant buries money given to him by his master so that he will be sure not to lose any. In contrast, his two fellow servants invest their money and thereby increase it. When the master discovers how the three men have used their bounty, he fires the fearful servant and gives the buried money to the other two. The moral of the story is that we lose what we don't use fruitfully. In today's economy, burying money is perhaps the equivalent of keeping money in a shoebox under the bed or even piling it up in a low-interest "savings" account—in essence, burying your money for fear of losing it or not having enough when you may need it.

Giving to others requires trusting that the flow will return to us. If we are too afraid to use what we have, but instead bury it without investing in others—or, for that matter, in ourselves—we may well find ourselves in the position of the first servant.

If we feel we do not have enough to give to others, we may indeed find ourselves having to go without. This does not mean that we should not save, but saving wisely and preparing for the future can mean trusting life enough to share and invest wisely.

If the inflow of prosperity is not balanced with an outflow of giving, the result will be stagnation. Any effort to hoard money cut off the dynamic flow of life.

As We Give

A dear friend of mine has had the pleasure and privilege of working closely with Donald Trump. She describes him as exuding a genuine love for life and, most strikingly, for people. He is a warm and passionate man who acknowledges the good around him. She recently met up with him in a limousine as they headed from the airport on their way to a speaking engagement that she had arranged. As they rode together, they discussed the talk that he was preparing to give to tens of thousands of people. Just outside the airport, they spotted a small group of young people who were waving and yelling, trying to get his attention. Trump asked his driver to stop so that he could meet them.

My friend expected him to open the window and wave. Instead, he got out of the car and spent several minutes signing autographs and sharing words of advice and encouragement, urging the kids to persist and to keep going for their goals. It was a touching moment for my friend. She already knew that Trump was generous with financial giving, but in this small but heartfelt gesture, she saw a man who genuinely appreciates what he has and is generous with something that is precious to all of us— time. A life of prosperity shows in the ways we give back, sometimes on a moment-by-moment basis.

HOW CAN YOU GIVE BACK?

Joyce Shirley volunteers once a week at a church pantry in South Carolina. Her 16-year-old niece Libby volunteers there, too. "We provide canned and dry food, plus fresh vegetables from local gardens. It's set up like a grocery store. We never send anyone away," Joyce explains. "I do it because I love the people. Where I live, there are so many people who'd simply go hungry without it—seniors and people who've lost their jobs. They're very appreciative. It makes me feel good to help."

Small Changes

Whether or not we are aware of it, when we give to others, that giving helps us move forward in life. Giving is a way to eliminate stagnation and stalled progress in your life, no matter what the cause of that stagnation. If your life is not flowing well and your circumstances are not what you desire, that is a perfect time to discover how you can give more to others. Doing so can renew your energy, inspiration, and motivation. Giving to others is a surefire way to know that you are making a difference and having a positive effect. Even if, at first, your giving is primarily intended to get your own life going, eventually it will become self-perpetuating. You'll find that you're giving to others simply because it feels good. You'll begin to give with no thought of reward. The funny thing is, the reward will never be far behind. What we give always comes back.

A common cause of stagnation, financial and otherwise, is a sense of entitlement. An attitude that life or others should provide for us can keep us stuck and is usually accompanied by a lack of gratitude for, and joy in, what we receive. The money may still come in, but the ability to truly enjoy and share the wealth will be diminished. Simple humility and respect for the value, intelligence, and potential of others is the antithesis of entitlement and opens the flow of abundance.

You can give to everyone you encounter, in ways both large and small, starting with a heartfelt compliment or a generous act of kindness. Begin with more smiles or more courtesy and care for others. To build your self-confidence and the ability to create abundance, move out of your comfort zone. Experiment with giving in a way that requires you to step up. Even a small change can make a big difference. And however you give, always know that it will increase your sense of prosperity and wealth because giving is inherently enriching. Because we are all connected, giving in any way is ultimately also a gift to oneself.

Increasing Self-Esteem by Fulfilling a Trust

Generosity should not mean being carefree with what we have, but rather being willing to support and empower others—and to give in ways that are constructive and that support the recipient's self-esteem. Ideally, this means giving others a hand up, not just a handout. Although there is a time for each of these types of giving, perhaps the best gift we can give others is to help them become more capable and independent. If our gifts are given in the spirit of helping others take a step forward in life, it opens the door to greater abundance for all concerned.

Perhaps the best gift we can give others is to help them become more capable and independent.

Giving freely and receiving with gratitude enrich our lives. Life improves exponentially when we understand that the more we give, the more we will receive. I have observed that the universe gives back whatever we give many times over, especially when we give with an open heart and no strings attached. We become prosperous through our generosity. A gift that is given unconditionally, with gratitude, empowers both the giver and the receiver. It mutually enhances self-worth and conveys a sense of trust to the person who receives it. To give to another unconditionally says that the recipient is valued, respected, and worthy of the gift. It's an acknowledgment of the other's being and the significance of that person's life or cause.

Genuine wealth has a sense of service at its core. As prosperity increases, a balanced life calls for one's service to also increase. In other words, to stay in harmony and balance, the greater the inflow, the greater the outflow must be.

Genuine wealth has a sense of service at its core. As prosperity increases, a balanced life calls for one's service to also increase.

As a youth, I certainly had little or no understanding of the principle that giving brings true prosperity. As far as I was concerned, the purpose of the money I earned was to serve my own needs. I was not a selfish person by nature, but an understanding of the benefits of giving had never been a focus in my life. It was years before I realized that achieving financial wealth is a hollow success unless it's a shared success. For me, there was no specific turning point for this realization. It emerged slowly through years of personal seasoning and observation. I came to understand that to give freely and with gratitude is also giving to oneself—for gifts cannot help but return to the giver.

I'm Going Through a Phase

*We are given one life and the decision is
ours whether to wait for circumstances to
make up our mind or whether to act, and in
acting, to live.*

—General Omar Bradley

For the first 10 years of his career, Michael Stern essentially followed in his father's footsteps. "My dad didn't like his job. His work was only a means to make a living and to provide for us. So it was not through my family that I learned about creating a rewarding life," Michael told me. Although he had a job that might be the envy of many, and a salary to match, Michael began to realize that he wanted something more from his work and his life. He explained it this way: "Figuring out what I really wanted to do took me several years of doing something I didn't enjoy. I was a computer and systems analyst on Wall Street. I was in my mid-thirties, and I knew I wanted to be a chiropractor.

"I decided to quit my job," he said. "It was a huge gamble at the time. After years of living a comfortable lifestyle, I became a student again. I had to take out loans in order to move and pay for school. I was scared. That was more than 20 years ago, and I haven't looked back." Since then, not only has Michael been a practicing chiropractor, but he has helped to pioneer cutting-edge techniques in the field. He says that reinventing himself in such a dramatic way was "the biggest, riskiest decision of my life, but I'm grateful that I dared to do it."

Dr. Michael Stern[1] was practicing in Minnesota when he heard about Mary. Her story illustrates what the world would have lost if Michael had not decided to reinvent his life. Because of a serious brain concussion, Mary had lost her ability to walk, talk, and function normally. She had been a writer, producer, and speaker when she was injured. While she was dining out with her family, a heavy lamp had hit her head. At first, the results were simply a large lump and a headache. But the next morning she woke up in terrible pain and with a level of dysfunction that was to keep her in bed for the next year, mostly sleeping or crying in pain. Her husband took her to neurologists; when they could not help, he started taking her to a variety of other practitioners. The appointments were too numerous to count, and only some of them were covered by insurance. After many months, Mary still could not walk unaided, and when she spoke, she made little or no sense. One year after the accident, the doctors told her husband that the brain damage was permanent.

Terribly concerned, a friend told Michael about Mary's condition. Michael volunteered to come to her home and examine her. With gentle techniques he had perfected and made his own, he worked with Mary. Each time he left, she was a little better. Within a few weeks, she was fully functional—in fact, she was even better than she had been before her accident. Michael's techniques seemed to have helped her brain to function even better than before. Math, which had once been her bane, was her new passion. Now fully recovered, she was participating with her family and in her community and went back to work.

Dr. Michael Stern is now a highly respected physician who has worked with thousands of grateful patients, including well-known athletes and celebrities. He is written about and sought after, and his unique techniques are taught at chiropractic colleges. The world is a better place for Michael's bet on himself.

Making Time

Time is a precious commodity these days. We never seem to have enough of it. One result is that it can be easy to get so caught up in life's daily demands that we don't take the time to orchestrate a life plan for ourselves—or even to plan from year to year. Often, we don't follow our dreams simply because we haven't thought about them. We don't take the time to build or create the life we want, let alone the time to appreciate the gifts we have.

MAKING IT REAL

Having passion is a great start, but it isn't enough. It's important that you create a specific goal and a plan for how to get there. Here are six action steps to help you get started:

- Put your passion in writing. Make it real.
- Think from the end. Visualize yourself living your dream. Then follow your steps backward to see how you got there.
- Take *Rich Dad, Poor Dad* author Robert Kiyosaki's advice: Don't say, "I can't afford it." Ask, "How can I afford it?"
- List three steps you can take immediately.
- List three steps you can take in the next month.
- Take action now!

If our attention is somewhere else, we miss the gift of our present experience. I recall that when I was a child, the days seemed long, and a year was like an endless stretch of road leading into the unknown. I realize today that this feeling of near-infinite time was the result of being fully present in the moment. We can experience the same sensation when we are fully engaged in doing something we love. Today, multitasking is the norm. Though electronic devices have their virtues, with all the gadgets we have available on which we can talk, text, browse, and play, the quiet moments to reflect seem ever more elusive. As a consequence, we are chronically distracted and inattentive. As time races ahead, life seems to pass us by.

Whatever we place our attention on will naturally grow. If we want to create prosperity, we must give it some conscious attention. The starting point is to take a serious look at the whole of our lives. This can help us understand not only where we are now, but what we have accomplished and where we want to go.

People typically look at their lives in terms of the chronological stages of physical life: birth, childhood, growing up, and aging. Of course, these general stages don't capture the infinite variety of human experience that each stage may include; each person's life is complex and unique. Yet each of us encounters certain cycles of experience that are universal. These cycles include financial ones—also known as "ups and downs"—during which our relationship with money can grow and evolve.

The Four Phases of Life

I characterize the four phases of life as Learning, Creating, Perfecting, and Freedom. These cycles aren't necessarily tied to a particular stage of life, such as growing up or growing old. They may march in sequence with our age, or they may be repeated many times in a single lifetime. They may even overlap. They reflect the fluidity of life and the ways in which we can—and sometimes must—start over, reinvent ourselves and our financial lives, and remain open to opportunities and challenges.

Learning

The *Learning* phase is the period in our lives when we are beginning something entirely new and have the innocence of the beginner. Like a young child, we are open and taking in everything. We are like sponges, absorbing new information that will prepare us for what comes next. In chronological terms, our first experience with this phase includes the years from birth to around age eight, when we are taking in information about the world at a rapid rate but are not yet exercising discrimination about what we're learning. We are still dependent on others and are not yet ready to make major decisions for ourselves. From age eight to eighteen, we continue to learn and absorb rapidly, but our powers of discrimination and decision making grow as we prepare for the next phase of life. When seen through a financial lens, the Learning phase can happen several, or even many, times in life—such as when we are starting a new job, career, or business, or when we are taking on a new responsibility that requires preparation, like the birth of a child.

Creating

The *Creating* phase is marked by moving into the world and taking on new responsibilities. We are starting to build a life in which we can stand on our own. In this phase, we may lack the resources to make it entirely under our own steam. To prepare us for independence, we might need to receive some support from parents or to borrow money to get a leg up. Unless we have inherited funds, in this phase we work to earn money, establish ourselves, and start saving.

During this phase, consciously obtained debt allows us to do and acquire things that we need in order to move ahead, such as buying a car. We invest in ourselves and in our future. In chronological terms, this phase follows schooling; we start to achieve some real independence, such as moving out of our parents' home for the first time. Chronologically, this phase may last well into our thirties—or, just as with the Learning phase, it may be experienced later in life when we are starting a new career.

Perfecting

The *Perfecting* phase is the period when we are established in a path and are standing on our own. It is the prime period of the cycle of life, when we have mastered our work and we are producing and earning at our full potential. With the demands of the Creating phase behind us, we are expanding our prosperity by saving or investing for retirement or the next stage of life. Although we are still producing, we are enjoying the fruits of what we have accomplished so far. We are independent, and we are entirely responsible for our own financial well-being. In this phase, we are the ones who can help others, such as our children, by giving them a hand up in life. Chronologically, this phase encompasses one's forties and fifties, and possibly beyond.

Freedom

The *Freedom* phase represents liberation from the need to work full time. With this phase comes the freedom to choose what's next. This may mean time to garden and travel, devote ourselves to an important cause, or explore a new vocation or career. It may also mean simply being able to structure our days exactly as we wish. We reflect on what we have accomplished, and yet we may wish to try something new. This is the phase in which we might decide to volunteer at a local children's center or bring our life and career skills to an area in need or to devote more time to our family. The essence of this period is having greater freedom to make choices. Whether our means are modest or extraordinary, we make our way as we wish.

We can experience any of these phases at any time in our lives. For example, at any age, we may want or need to start a new career or a new adventure. It is no longer uncommon for people to begin a new job or career in any decade of life, including our sixties or older. When this happens, the entire cycle begins again. We once again experience the Learning phase and, if all goes well, move to the phase of Creating a new way of life, then on to Perfecting, where we become established in our new career. With each repetition of the cycle, we bring more experience, discipline, and focus to it than we did before. As we move into each new cycle, nothing in our experience is lost.

Today's world is an extremely fluid and dynamic place. "High-speed connection" not only captures the way in which many of us access the Internet, but also describes what is required if we are to keep pace with our own needs and the demands of a changing economy and culture. This high-speed connection is also an internal requirement. Staying true to what we want and need in the midst of rapid changes keeps us on the path to our personal goals of prosperity.

Understanding these phases allows us to use them to our advantage and to appreciate that our personal evolution never ends. Starting over is an opportunity to learn things about ourselves that, as Thomas Edison said, will astound us. If for no other reason, the occasional need to reinvent and reimagine ourselves—to stretch and find new pathways to a prosperous life—is something to embrace.

Genius in Boldness

I attended a speaking engagement at which a man told his story of self-reinvention and resourcefulness. The man and his wife, both in their fifties, were speaking to thousands of people about the loss of his longtime job in the recession that began in 2008. Because of his previous success and experience, he was confident that he would find a new position quickly. But two years went by in which he had no meaningful employment. Prospective employers told him that he was too old or that he was overqualified. In order to survive, he and his wife had exhausted their savings and depleted their credit. They had reached a stage where they were concerned about paying for food. All they had left was their house, and the proverbial wolves were at the door. Then the man heard about a sales opportunity that produced income strictly on commission. He was intrigued. The position required a relatively small investment of $500 for training. It would be his own business, and he liked that idea, too. He talked to his wife, but she was cautious.

At this point in his story, the man's wife shook her head and looked at him. She explained, "I saw absolutely no way he could start a new business, no matter how small the investment." She just wanted him to take any job with anyone who would have him. The day after her husband described the opportunity to her, she arrived home from work, weary from the day and the near-constant worry. She asked him why it was so cold in the house. "I sold the furnace," he said. "I got $500 for it."

At this, the audience erupted in laughter and simultaneously groaned. How could he have done that? What was he thinking? Then he told us, "I knew this was my chance. I had to act. We would be a little cold that winter, but I knew how to work hard and to sell, and the opportunity looked great." He apologized to all the wives in the audience, but he explained that his wife had since forgiven him many times over.

On stage that day, she was beautifully dressed and held a dozen red roses. His kids were there, too. He was now making more money than he had made in the original job that he had lost, and it had been less than a year since he had started. He had reached a level in sales that qualified him for this moment of acknowledgment. Something tells me that the first thing he did when the money started coming in was to buy his wife a nice new furnace.

What is extraordinary about this story is the man's audacity and courage—and his outrageous creativity and commitment. Although he wasn't chronologically young, he was thoroughly willing to start over and try again—and to take a certain amount of risk in doing so. He recognized his opportunity, and he took it. He didn't accept that he was too old to create something new. His relationship with money was obviously on a solid footing, and his self-respect was high. He spoke for only six minutes, but he received a standing ovation.

A Tale of Debt and Failure

When he was 22 years old, a young man lost his job—it seems that his boss was a lousy businessman. The young man had transported goods from his boss's store in Illinois to New Orleans, with the promise of running the business upon his return. His boss fulfilled the promise, and for the few months that he ran the business, the young man did a fine job. But the owner's financial troubles eventually caused the store to shut down. Our young fellow was out of a job. The following year, his friends encouraged him to run for a seat in the state legislature. He lost miserably, finishing eighth in a field of thirteen. He and a friend opened another store, but competition was too stiff, and this store also failed.

With no way to pay off his debts, our young man was in dire straits. The sheriff seized his possessions, and when his business partner died shortly thereafter, he decided to assume his partner's share of their debt as well. In debt and struggling, the young man worked diligently and succeeded in paying off everything that he owed. He attained a new position as local postmaster. But his real love was for the law. Throughout his travails, he had been studying for and ultimately passed the bar exam.

With his confidence renewed, he again ran for the legislature, and this time he won. A series of successes and failures came and went—including losing bids for the U.S. Congress and Senate—even as the man rose in his state's political hierarchy. In 1860, he was nominated and elected president of the United States. Such was the life of Abraham Lincoln. It was not a straight line through the phases of life, certainly, but it led to a career as one of the most revered presidents in America's history.

Always bear in mind that your own resolution to succeed is more important than any other one thing.

—Abraham Lincoln

Reinventing Your Life

It makes me smile just to think about Denise Fast. Denise is a poet. She has written 16 books of poetry, and she weaves her poems into talks at the many events at which she is invited to speak.

Her poetry tells the story of her life and, in so doing, hints at the depths and heights that we all experience. She is also a top broker in West Los Angeles and a go-to person for all matters regarding real estate. In fact, she is a go-to person for just about everything. Her phone rings constantly, and I'm sure to hear a celebrity's name if I sit in her office even for a little while. In a real estate downturn, she is still busy and successful. She has received sales awards for extraordinary achievement annually and has placed in the top 100 real estate agents internationally four times. Denise is also a generous person who finds many ways to assist others who are less fortunate than she. She understands their plight, because she's been there.

We all have a gift to give to the world—and a place where we can do our best work. Sometimes it takes patience and persistence to find that place. Fortunately, through the twists, turns, and phases of her life, Denise took the time to find her true place. Seeing her today, however, supporting and empowering so many others through her business, it's hard to imagine her in any other role.

"I was a single mom, struggling and waiting tables. In order to better support my daughter, I decided to make a shift from waitressing to getting a manicurist's license. This would allow me to work days instead of nights. The only way I could make it work was to go on welfare for a short period. The state paid for my schooling. Once I graduated, I got a terrific job and started to do well." Denise was grateful for the help. She went on to develop a large and loyal clientele and managed to put her daughter through private school on a manicurist's salary. She became entirely self-sufficient, and she remains thankful for the support she received along the way.

Today, Denise could still be one of the many single mothers who are waiting tables or doing nails and surviving from paycheck to paycheck. She didn't have a college education; in fact, she had barely finished high school. But she took the time to reflect and consider her dream. "I was at work as a manicurist in Santa Monica, when one day my new husband commented that I was really smart. He asked me, 'Why don't you do something that allows you to use your brain?'" Denise thought about it and recognized that she had always been very resourceful. She thought that perhaps she could help people find houses and even own one herself someday. With that realization, an exceptional real estate agent was born.

"Growing up, I watched my self-supporting mother lose a home to foreclosure. This was very painful, in part because I knew how important homeownership was to her." Denise continued tearfully, "When I was older, I wrote my mother a letter promising her that someday I would be successful and restore her to the lifestyle that she deserved. I folded the letter and placed it into the pages of a poetry book I had written. Then I mailed it to her as a gift."

SURVIVING LIFE

There are chapters of my life I'd like to overlook

Tear out the pages right from my book

But each one made me who I am today

They were written in love so others won't be afraid to say

This is what it took, the lessons I learned, along the way

—Denise Fast[2]

Several years ago, Denise was helping to pack her mother's belongings to move her mom to the new home that Denise had just bought for her. The poetry book that Denise had sent years earlier fell out of her mother's things, along with the letter. Perfect timing. With gratitude, Denise recognized that she had made not one, but two dreams come true—her own and her mom's.

Even knowing that purchasing and selling real estate could change her life for the better, Denise cried at the thought of leaving her clientele as a manicurist—the 40 loyal customers that she had befriended over the previous eight years. But she found the courage to push beyond her cozy world, go back to the beginning, and learn something entirely new. She and her husband, a general contractor, have now purchased and sold more than a dozen homes of their own. With all her success, Denise feels that her business is merely a platform to bring value to the lives of the people she serves—an expression of a true psychology of wealth.

Our Cousins, the Amoebas

What keeps us from realizing our personal dreams of fulfillment and success? From my observation, it's primarily fear and inertia. Fear of failure and of the unknown is human and universal. What we do in the face of that fear either keeps us locked in one life phase or propels us to a more fulfilling life.

Inertia can result from an overattachment to our comfort zone. Many of us won't stray far beyond that zone unless we are forced to, either by events or by some threat to our well-being. The avoidance of pain or discomfort will often push us forward, but as life strategies go, pain avoidance is less than ideal.

Life is a process of becoming, a combination of states we have to go through. Where people fail is that they wish to elect a state and remain in it. —Anaïs Nin

During an undergraduate biology class, I had the opportunity to observe amoebas under a microscope. The behavior of these tiny single-celled organisms was fascinating. They seemed to be entirely governed by their responses to external stimuli. Without fail, they moved away from any unfavorable stimulus and toward any desirable one. As B. F. Skinner would say, this was "operant conditioning" at its finest—a primitive but effective survival mechanism that is purely instinctual. I wondered: as human beings, how different are we from the amoebas?

One of our unique abilities is the power to override such instincts, either to our benefit or to our detriment. In my private practice as a psychotherapist, I've seen this at work many times. When people are stuck in dysfunctional reactive patterns or relationships, they often remain in an undesirable situation rather than doing something that might bring them relief and comfort, or even pleasure. Since we can override our natural survival instincts to avoid pain and discomfort, our inertia suggests that we are sometimes even less adaptive than the lowly amoeba.

Some people are highly motivated to do more, be more, and stretch beyond the point of comfort. Bravo! However, for a person in whom that high level of motivation is not inherent, new learning and behavior may come only when the discomfort of remaining stuck is greater than that of learning something new. Somewhere along the way, such a person has lost, or hasn't yet found, the impulse inherent in all life to discover new things and even to face new challenges.

People who have a psychology of wealth challenge themselves to move beyond their comfort zone to pursue a goal or a dream. They write down goals. They plan. They visualize. Like brave children intent on conquering the world, they move beyond mere reactions and old patterns to face challenges and the unknown. Even if some people seem to have lost this spirit of openness—and, well, fun—they need not be completely adrift. The childlike part of adults that loves to learn is still inside each of us, and the successful people are the ones who harness it. We can go beyond the amoebic approach to life. We can recapture our enthusiasm for moving toward what we desire, as opposed to merely avoiding what we don't want.

Even as you read these pages, you've probably thought of certain things that you could do—of dreams, goals, or opportunities that you've wanted to realize. When are you going to start? When will you begin to manifest your dreams? Why not today? Why not this very moment? Even a small step is a start. In fact, a series of small steps may get you where you are going more quickly than a giant leap, and sometimes with fewer bruises. The first step may not be easy, but it's important to take it. As Tony Cupisz says, "To find success, you have to do something every day. Just do something!"

Whose Job Is This, Anyway?

Most of us have gone through periods of financial challenge and struggle—times when we have no idea how we will get from point A to point B. Things usually seem to work out in the end, but when we are in the thick of the difficulty, we often imagine the worst. I've observed that life never presents us with an unsolvable problem. The solution may humble us or require us to do things that we've never done before, but there is always a solution.

A series of small steps may get you where you are going more quickly than a giant leap, and sometimes with fewer bruises.

During graduate school, I worked at a psychiatric hospital for three years. The rate of patient recidivism made it feel as if the hospital had a giant revolving door. Mental health patients would be treated and discharged, only to return weeks later. During my last year there, I began to feel that my efforts at the hospital had no real value or significance. I wanted out, but where was I to go? Since I needed to make a living, I wondered what other employment I could find that might be relevant to my training. As I contemplated this puzzle, I realized that it might take a while before I could change my job, and I might as well make the best of what I had in the meantime. I decided to notice the aspects of the job and my patients that I genuinely appreciated. My idea was to bring more meaning to my work.

The moment I began to practice appreciation, things started to change. Not only did my attitude improve, but a short time later I was offered a paid counseling internship at a new clinic near campus. Had my change of attitude profoundly changed my world? Perhaps. I was certainly grateful for the opportunity that the new position afforded me. It was an ideal next step for me, and it prepared me for the private practice that I opened after I received my doctorate.

Ideally, our work is both lucrative and a way to express meaning in our lives. Yet if it isn't, we can still learn and grow wherever we are. By applying the principles of the Learning phase—being open to new ideas and ways of seeing our world—we can begin anew even in our current situation. We can also re-examine our values and interests and look for opportunities to follow our nose and our dreams. This is what Michael Stern and Denise Fast finally did. And this is what Jane Pulkys did too.

Rewriting Your Life

My friend Jane is a petite blonde with a big personality. She was 39 years old when her husband's company had a massive layoff, and overnight her family went from a six-figure income to having nothing whatsoever. "It was several long years before our family of five would see a paycheck again," Jane told me. "We sold the 'big' house and used our savings to pay bills. We scaled back. We got by."

Jane had been a stay-at-home mom with three boys, but now it was time for her to dust off the enterprising person she had been as a young girl. Growing up in Ontario in a family of nine, Jane had started working when she was quite young. "I always understood that there really wasn't extra money in the household. I took it upon myself to get my first job when I was 11. I was responsible for my own money, and I also had to give some of it to my mother to help support the family."

In college, Jane earned a degree in nutrition, but after graduation, she decided to dedicate herself fully to starting and raising a family. When her husband lost his job, she had to look at different possibilities for work. "One day I took my friend to visit a clinic that offered specialized nutrition counseling. By the time we left, I just knew this was what I needed to do."

Jane continued, "There was so much to do. I had to really stretch, but I am so glad I did. I scheduled a trip to take a course from the top practitioner in the field, and I also had to buy some rather expensive equipment. The following year I opened my own practice. Because I still wanted and needed additional training and education, I went back to school at night for two years and worked during the day. Once I'd received my degree as a holistic nutritionist, I pushed myself to contact television stations about the innovative work I was doing, and I was invited to appear on a morning TV show. The day I did, the floodgates opened. I had no idea I would have so many people wanting appointments. Since then, I've appeared on television and been interviewed on radio many times, and my practice continues to thrive."

True wealth is having a job that you love so much, you don't realize you are actually working. —Jane Pulkys

---

In short, out of necessity and desire, Jane rewrote her life and far surpassed her own expectations. "The changes I made have allowed me to teach wellness seminars at Fortune 500 companies and to develop a holistic psychology of disease course. Recently I was invited to teach my course in Thailand. I'm helping others, and I love that." In the process, Jane's idea of wealth has also been rewritten. "True wealth is having the love and support of my family and friends, certainly. But I've learned something else, too. True wealth is having a job that you love so much, you don't realize you are actually working. I go to bed every night thinking, 'I have made a difference in someone's life today.' The bonus is that I get paid for it."

A WORD FROM THE WISE

In *It Is What It Is: The Personal Discourses of Rumi*, author and speaker Doug Marman retells a Rumi tale about our individual purpose in the world: "There is one thing in this world that must never be forgotten. If you were to forget all else, but did not forget that, then you would have no reason to worry. But if you performed and remembered everything else, yet forgot that one thing, then you would have done nothing whatsoever.

"It is just as if a king sent you to the country to carry out a specific task. If you go and accomplish a hundred other tasks, but do not perform that one task, then it is as though you performed nothing at all. So, everyone comes into this world for a particular task, and that is their purpose. If they do not perform it, then they will have done nothing."[3]

Time to Smell the Roses

The Freedom phase of financial life, in which a job or a career is no longer required to support our prosperity, is a golden goal for most of us. Having the freedom to apply our attention, energy, and love to an endeavor of our choosing is a gift that we will have earned well when it arrives. For many people, this idea may seem like an impossibility. And, indeed, especially during tough economic times, achieving it may be more of a challenge than ever. But that doesn't mean that we have to put off many aspects of this prosperous state until our later years. We can appreciate what we have and feel a sense of satisfaction in what we have achieved right here and now by consciously living in the moment and accepting each day as priceless. Far from being old-fashioned, the needlepoint advice to stop and smell the roses is timeless. Ah, sweet, sweet rose—perhaps it's time for us to take a break and appreciate you.

More and more people are finding themselves in the position of needing—or wanting—to begin anew and reinvent a life that they had thought was settled and satisfactory. If the need comes unexpectedly and even with some distress, it can still be a great opportunity to ride an upward spiral to an even more prosperous life.

Our economy and the dynamic nature of our society today require flexibility and fluidity and recognition that life can be rejuvenated again and again. We can use this fluidity to our great advantage. Even when opportunities may seem limited, we have wells of invention and creativity within us. With openness, consciousness, and a willingness to work and focus on our goals, we can achieve prosperity.

After all, it's not the pursuit of wealth that brings value and meaning to life; it's the pursuit of meaning and value that brings wealth. This wealth is greater than a full bank account. It's the wealth that is experienced by living a life of quality, joy, service, and fulfillment. This is the true wealth that we all ultimately seek to achieve. Anything less leaves us hungry for more.

Painting a New Portrait of Prosperity

There are no accidents . . . there is only some purpose that we haven't yet understood.

—Deepak Chopra

Can one person actually embody the psychology of wealth? Can he do so even if he is neither a millionaire nor wealthy by most monetary standards? Dennis Gardin is a great example of someone who can.

When his motorcycle blew up in his face, Dennis was 14 years old and living in Detroit. Against his parents' wishes, he and some friends had sneaked the bike into the basement for repairs. The boys didn't notice how close they were to the furnace. Gasoline leaked out, ran under the hot water heater, and caught fire. Three of the four boys, including Dennis, ran out of the basement to safety. When Dennis realized that his other friend was still inside, he ran back in.

"When I got in the basement, I found my friend looking at the fire and screaming. He wasn't burned. But when I grabbed him, he turned and jumped on my back in a panic. As I was trying to get him off, the motorcycle exploded. The entire front side of my body was burned. Because he was on my back, my body shielded part of his body." Dennis woke up in a hospital burn ward with 70 percent of his body burned. He recalled, "My friend, who was burned on 20 percent of his body, had been transferred to the children's hospital. I was too unstable to be transported. They didn't expect me to survive, so it didn't really matter where I died."

Following the explosion, Dennis spent eight months in the hospital, where he endured 50 surgeries. "I had skin graft after skin graft, and significant reconstructive work. As soon as my mind would clear from the anesthesia, I'd be on my way back to the operating room. That's all I did. This certainly wasn't part of my 14-year-old plan. I was going to be a baseball player. This was a serious inconvenience for me—to go from playing ball and running up and down the street with my friends to endless surgeries and months in a hospital bed."

Today Dennis is executive director of the Georgia Firefighters Burn Foundation.[1] He and the foundation help burn survivors in their recovery and provide fire safety education to prevent others from experiencing the traumatic event of a burn injury.

GIVE THANKS

Every day for a week, write down five things for which you are grateful. Observe how it makes you feel.

From Dennis's story and the stories of the many other people whom I met and interviewed, a portrait of human prosperity had emerged—an inner richness that surpasses any other kind of wealth. Their prosperity seems to come from several essential qualities. Among them is a willingness to face challenges and setbacks, turn them into opportunities, and find meaning in the challenge. Their prosperity also stems from a willingness to take responsibility and face life creatively, to find solutions, and not to accept less than all they can give.

Like Dennis Gardin, these resourceful people know that whatever their circumstances or backgrounds may be, it's up to no one but themselves to create their lives. They are true to their unique set of values. Like many of the people described in this book, they have the courage to discover and then to follow their individual dreams.

These people have adopted a psychology of wealth. In so doing, they have plugged into the evolutionary impulse, inherent in all human beings, to expand and grow. There is something of the seeker in these prosperous souls. Like Representative Johnny Shaw, they take a view of life that demands an appreciation of the little things. They are grateful. They take steps, and even risks, to move themselves forward. In the process, they accrue self-esteem and self-respect. And they're persistent about it. They are willing to stand and fight. Like Senator Van de Putte, when called upon, they step up. They flow with the twists and turns in the stream of life. And like Bennie Taylor, who fought in Vietnam, they are willing to serve others, yet ask for help when they need it.

In turn, they are generous, supportive, and thankful for what they have and what they've achieved. They face life with grace and withstand the storms of change, loss, and discrimination. They bring consciousness to their actions and decisions. They're honest with themselves and alert to life's possibilities. And they are willing to do whatever it takes to succeed—even in the face of unspeakable pain and fear.

I Am a Monster

"When I was in the hospital," Dennis reflected, "and we're talking 40 years ago now, this burn unit was a single ward, where all the patients were in a room together, men and women. I was the only kid in the unit. One of the most difficult things for me was hearing adults crying in pain. I didn't know adults cried like that. I thought, 'If adults can't deal with this, what am I going to do as a 14-year-old?'

"The ward wasn't designed to address the needs of a kid. However, the staff did certain things for me—I guess because I was such a darn sweet kid," he joked. "They changed my dressings each day before everyone else, so I wouldn't have to anticipate my turn while hearing the screams of the other patients. That may seem like a small thing, but it wasn't," he said.

"There were no mirrors in the burn unit. My knowledge of reconstructive surgery was limited to movie stars, and they always came out looking better. Whenever the doctors took off my bandages, they'd comment about how good I looked. In a weird way, I actually thought I must look better than before. I mean, no one in my life had ever stood over me saying how good I looked," he said ruefully. "One day, after many months of this, my mom and my brother were walking me down the hall, and I caught a clear reflection of myself in a glass door. I lost it. It truly scared me. That couldn't be me. I was a monster.

"I collapsed and lay in the hallway, screaming that I wanted to die. They had to sedate me and my mom." Dennis continued, "Oh, man, it was a mess. After that, I didn't think that life could get any worse—until I was discharged. I was so ashamed of how I looked. I went home and hid. I refused to go out. Tutors came to the house for my schooling. But the most difficult part was seeing my parents helpless for the first time. They didn't know what to do. Every night my earnest prayer was that I would die in my sleep. Then every morning I'd wake up with a broken heart because I'd woken up."

Dennis now teaches the kids with whom he works that they are not burn *victims*—they are burn *survivors*. This empowering concept encompasses not only the person who is burned, but everyone in the family who was touched by the event. "The family members are injured as well," he explained, "emotionally and even spiritually. They are all burn survivors.

"All my parents wanted was for me to be okay. I had been hiding at home for two years. When I finally decided to leave the house, it was more about them than about me. I felt that if I went back to school and got a diploma like a normal kid, it would be a gift to my parents. It would say, 'I'm okay. Your efforts were worth it.' But the truth is that I was scared to death."

Multiplying by 10

"When I went to school," Dennis continued, "everything I feared became a reality. It was much more difficult than I thought it would be. The teachers sat me at the back of the class so people wouldn't look at me, and they dismissed me from class early, so I could escape the crowded halls. They did all the wrong things for the right reasons. The first time I went into the lunchroom and sat down, a girl jumped up and screamed, 'How dare you come in here and spoil everyone's appetite?' I would come home every day and lock myself in the bathroom to cry.

"Eventually I realized that the more I tried to hide, the worse it got. So I figured, 'If I'm going to be noticed, let's just put it out there. Let's just do it.'"

A shift had occurred inside him. Dennis had learned about positive thinking techniques from his baseball coaches. He began to remember these lessons. "When I was an athlete, the coaches would always say, 'You've got to believe in yourself. Visualize hitting the ball over the fence, and tell yourself you're the best player on the field.' I transferred that idea to my situation. Every day, I counted how many times people talked badly about me or treated me unfairly. Then at night, I multiplied that number by 10. That was the number of times I would say to myself, 'I love me,' while I stood in front of a mirror. I would say it over and over. At some point I started to believe it."

RECLAIM YOUR POWER

Pay attention to your

- Thoughts

- Words

- Actions

- Beliefs

Keep them positive.

"Mind you, I wasn't deliberately applying positive thinking principles," explained Dennis. "I was still struggling. I was just a kid trying to survive. But once my appearance was no longer an issue for me, it seemed like it was no longer an issue for other people. I began to notice that not everybody was acting negatively toward me. Because I had expected negativity, that was the message I was sending out, and those were the cues I was picking up on." He started participating in extracurricular activities and went to all the school games. In his senior year, he ran for class president and came in second. He got his diploma and graduated at the top of his class.

"I was born into a close-knit, very loving family. They are all about acceptance—about accepting who you are. Those principles buoyed me up. When I gave the diploma to my mom, my grandma grabbed it, she was so excited."

Dennis realized that he could not hide any longer. Comparing himself to the hunchback of Notre Dame, he explained, "After I graduated, I couldn't go back into my room, like Quasimodo in the bell tower. That was no longer an option."

Dennis went to college, became a hospital administrator, and eventually started a successful music business. He was also married for a while. He wanted a normal life, and he refused to be identified with his burns. "I wasn't going to be a burn person. I spent a good deal of my adult life trying to be normal, and I was fairly successful with it. But I wasn't happy. I didn't even know what 'happy' meant. I knew I should be grateful for what I had, so how could I not be happy?

"My entire life changed when I got a phone call from a friend with whom I'd worked at the hospital. Her uncle had been burned, and he was deeply depressed. She said, 'Dennis, could you go talk to him? We don't know what else to do.' Because I was busy and distracted, I just wanted to hang up, so I told her I would do it. Immediately afterward, I went into a panic. Why did I tell her yes? Then I got mad. What right did she have to ask me to do this? But, really, I was scared. What was I going to talk about with this guy?" That fateful phone call came 23 years after Dennis had been burned.

He gathered his courage and went to the hospital. "It was my first time in a burn unit as a nonpatient." When the doors to the unit opened, he broke into a cold sweat and nearly fainted. But he met the man he had come to visit. "I don't remember what we talked about, but at the end, he thanked me and asked me to extend his appreciation to the support group for sending me. I was confused. There was a support group? I still had never spoken with another person outside of a hospital who'd been burned. But for the first time, something good had come from my experience. This man appreciated our conversation, and I'd learned that other people who'd been burned actually got together and talked about it. I learned that there was a group that met once a month a couple of miles from where I worked. But I didn't go.

"Sometime later, the wife of the burned man called to ask if I would speak with his coworkers to prepare them for his coming back to work. Overcoming my extreme reluctance again, I went to the man's workplace. The guys there expressed their appreciation for my coming, and a man asked, 'Do you talk to schools? I know a kid who was burned and is having a hard time.' I opened my mouth to say no—and again, yes came out." Next, Dennis was invited to speak to an entire school. Other teachers attended and invited him to their schools.

It's impossible to extend oneself from a place of purity and goodness to help another person without being helped in the process.   —Dennis Gardin

---

Thankful in All Things

"I finally went to that support group," said Dennis. "As I listened to nine other burn survivors, I realized I had finally found another family—a group of people who not only knew how I felt, but felt the same way. I wasn't alone anymore. From them, I learned about a conference of several hundred burn survivors, to be held in San Francisco."

When Dennis arrived at the conference, he was too terrified to go in. The chairperson, a retired firefighter and burn survivor, took him aside and got Dennis to tell him his story. He gently encouraged Dennis to attend a session. Soon thereafter, Dennis entered the session room, and the chairperson announced that the first speaker hadn't shown up. When he recalled the moment, Dennis laughed. The next thing he heard from the podium was, "But I met a young man who has a story I thought was amazing, and I think you guys are going to find it amazing, too." Dennis was called to the stage—and he went. "I cried my way through a 30-minute presentation that ended in a standing ovation. Before that conference was over, organizations from different parts of the globe had asked me to come talk to them. And the telephone hasn't stopped ringing since."

Dennis is now a happy man. "Through extending myself to help someone else, I was helped in the process," he explained. "It's a universal principle, like a personal law—it's impossible to extend oneself from a place of purity and goodness to help another person without being helped in the process.

"I speak because my heart says that's what I have to do. As a motivational speaker, I've now traveled around the world several times." He recently addressed the first adult burn survivor retreats in Australia and in South Africa. "The decisions I made from the time of that first phone call were really about allowing myself to follow my path. Odessa Scott, my grandmother, used to come to the hospital every day and rub my feet for hours, just praying and thanking. I couldn't understand how she could be giving thanks. For what? She said, 'Baby, you have to be thankful *in* all things, not thankful *for* all things. God's not punishing you. God is preparing you to do your work.'

Baby, you have to be thankful in *all things, not thankful*
for all things. —Odessa Scott

"It was years before I understood what she was talking about—that the incident (I can't call it an accident) was meant to happen so that I could receive the gifts of those experiences. And so that when a kid is telling me what he's going through, and I say, 'I know,' he knows that I do."

Dennis's insight into the psychology of wealth is profound. He has learned firsthand that it is our responses to life's challenges that determine our level of prosperity and the richness of our lives. "I've learned to accept that I can't change other people's responses to me. All I can do is to accept other people, stay open, and respond the way I would want others to respond to me."

As for wealth itself, Dennis says, "Wealth is having a life of purpose and being able to fulfill that purpose—being able to make a difference in someone else's life. In the time I have left on this planet, I want to start seeing burn survivors communicate with each other and their loved ones about their feelings and experiences, so they can truly heal and get on with their own lives." If they can get on with their lives the way Dennis Gardin has, the world will be a much richer place.

Fire and Power

Dennis touches the lives of hundreds of children every year, helping them to heal from their own burn experiences. Joey Wincek is one of those "kids." Now in his twenties, Joey was just seven years old when he started going to burn camp[2] every summer. Now he gives back as a camp counselor. Little kids surround him as he arrives at the camp, yelling, "Joey, Joey, Joey!" and he smiles hugely down at them from his six-foot three-inch frame.

He was burned as a baby; he was playing and splashing in the tub when the water suddenly turned scalding. He was laughing and happy one moment and fighting for his life the next. His burns were deep and required agonizing surgeries. Joey attributes his ability to get through the pain and his difficult teenage years to the love and support of his family and of Dennis. On his forearms are two tattoos with Chinese symbols that mean "power" and "fire." "Power," Joey explains, "is about knowing what you have to do and doing it. It is about claiming your life and assuming the responsibility. And fire? It's about passion—finding what you love and giving it your all." For him, the tattoos mean that he is in charge of his own skin.

Joey is now in an internship at Georgia Institute of Technology and is living a productive and happy life, following his passion. And although a third of his body is badly scarred, his heart is in perfect working order and full of love.

First, You Get the Moon

Stuart Johnson couldn't wait to get started in life. The product of an upper-middle-class family, he could have had an exceptionally easy route to prosperity. But he had a strong independent streak. He felt an inner command to take a different path and to make something unique for himself—and as soon as possible. Stuart wanted to be an entrepreneur. And so, at a young age and on his own, he started his first business.

Today, not only does Stuart own a huge media company, but he moves among CEOs, celebrities, opinion leaders, and politicians—some very successful people indeed. He has built a business empire on his passion for achievement. Very successful himself, he loves encouraging success in others. It is fitting, then, that he is the owner of *SUCCESS* magazine. *SUCCESS* lives up to its name. Its covers are graced by people who have made unique contributions and achievements in their respective fields:

Steve Jobs, Mark Zuckerberg, Usher, Maria Shriver, Jackie Chan, Alicia Keys, and Magic Johnson, to name a few. The magazine is one way in which Stuart shares what he and other highly accomplished people have learned along the way. His tenacity is an example in itself. "I had wanted to own the magazine for over a decade," he says. "I always knew that if I did what I needed to do, somehow the opportunity for me to purchase it would arise. I kept working at it, and, just over four years ago, the opportunity came."

Never quit, never surrender, never give up, never, never, never. —Winston Churchill

---

Stuart's formula for success? "Hard work, hard work, and just showing up!" He took his lumps along the way. "Once I got started, I began to make money very quickly. But I might have had a taste of success too early. I started believing my press a little bit more than I should have, and I became overconfident. I guess I had to get a couple of rocks thrown at me before I realized what it really takes to succeed." He got knocked down—and more than once. He admits that he failed at least six or seven times before the age of 21. Of course, most people are barely getting started at that age, and Stuart was already rebuilding. "When I had gone down for the fourth or fifth time, my mom finally said, 'Stop trying to take the easy road. Just get a job!' But the setbacks had only fired me up and confirmed my conviction that I wanted to be an entrepreneur. Somehow I knew I'd make it and become successful." To Stuart, failing is not a bad thing. It's just an indication that he needs to try another avenue. "After 25 years, I'm an overnight success," he laughs.

STUART JOHNSON'S BOOK GUIDE

Reading books with positive messages can change your thinking and your life. When Stuart Johnson was 15, reading these three books changed his:

Think and Grow Rich, by Napoleon Hill

The Magic of Thinking Big, by David J. Schwartz

Success Through a Positive Mental Attitude, by Napoleon Hill and W. Clement Stone

He recommends these books to start with today:

The Compound Effect, by Darren Hardy

The Slight Edge, by Jeff Olson

Surrounded by extremely successful people—and being one himself—Stuart often works outside the spotlight. With his lightning-quick and quiet intelligence, he is an intuitive observer of psychological strengths in people who have reached their goals with more than usual success. "Successful people, like Donald Trump, Suze Orman, and Oprah Winfrey, have tenacity. They can be knocked down, but they're not knocked out. They have integrity, and they work hard. They put good people around them, and they always seem to really care about others." Stuart expresses these qualities himself: "I'm just grateful for everything I've been able to accomplish, for all the people I've been able to touch. I have a great family, a great network of friends, and a great team. I feel blessed just to wake up and be able to do business and have fun with them. I think a wealthy life is knowing you are doing the best you can to make a difference."

Stuart advises anyone who wants to take the next step toward prosperity: "If you shoot for the stars and actually hit the moon, it's a start. It's a lot better than not trying. You have to be realistic; you can't just wake up and say, 'I'm going to be a billionaire by Friday.' At the same time, it's just as easy to have big goals as it is to have small goals. But it's not just going to come to you. You still have to get up and take action."

The Call

Surrounded by young kids who are trying to make it up a ropes challenge course, Joey Wincek is encouraging them. It is not easy to face life with the added challenge of serious scars. But here at burn camp, in the middle of a Georgia pine forest, everyone is going for it. They are being encouraged and cheered on to achieve things that many of us would not be able to handle. It's nearly 100 degrees outside, but no one seems to notice. The kids are all lining up to tackle the high ropes. Using harnesses, helmets, cables, ropes, nets, and wooden beams strung high among the trees and poles, the kids explore risk taking, trust, and mutual coaching. Some are struggling, and sweat pours from their faces. The hydration team stands ready to provide water whenever it's needed. But the kids don't back down. They have come to face the challenge. Joey likes sports metaphors, so he describes it this way: "It's not about being on the sidelines," he says. "This is your life, and you're supposed to be a player, on the field and fully engaged."

It's not about being on the sidelines. This is your life, and you're supposed to be a player, on the field and fully engaged.   —Joey Wincek

---

"We're all called," Oprah Winfrey says. She asserts that each of us has a role to play in the world. She continues, "If you're here breathing, you have a contribution to make to our human community. The real work of your life is to figure out your function—your part in the whole—as soon as possible and then get about the business of fulfilling it as only you can."[3] Representative Johnny Shaw would say that it's about being "obedient to your purpose."

Dennis Gardin and Stuart Johnson provide two very different portraits of prosperity. And yet it strikes me that a common quality shines through both of them. Taking different routes—and at different times in their lives—each man found the purpose to which he was called. In the process, each of them created a fulfilling life. Joey Wincek might say that they are in their power. They show us that when we are in our power—in touch with and aligned with our calling—good things tend to happen. When we strive for what is important to us as individuals, then opportunities arise, and the chances to share with others become abundant. Life becomes connected and dramatically sensible. When it happens, we just know, "I'm in the right place, doing the right thing. I'm where I know I was meant to be." When we find our calling, the special something that really inspires us, we can achieve more than we ever imagined.

I think Oprah puts it best, and it's one of the things that she says she knows for sure: "There is no greater gift you can give or receive than to honor your calling. It's why you were born. And how you become most truly alive."[4]

Knowing Where to Plant Your Feet

*We cannot solve our problems with
the same thinking we used when we
created them.*

—Albert Einstein

Deep within the University of Tennessee is a professor's small office, crammed with books and papers, and decorated with photos of black cultural luminaries. I had made my way there through a blizzard to talk with its occupant. When I arrived, in the parking space reserved for him, I found a fully loaded red Honda Valkyrie motorcycle.

The office and motorcycle belong to Harold Black, Ph.D., the eminent finance educator, from whom I was to learn much about consumer choice. When I met him on that winter day, he was dressed in a white shirt, a blue sport coat, and a red plaid bow tie. He is highly distinguished, outspoken, and down to earth. Apparently, Dr. Black is also a jazz aficionado: the pictures on his walls are of jazz masters Miles Davis and Thelonious Monk. He is a master of finance: a list of his accomplishments, positions, and writings requires 23 pages. They include his appointment as a board member of the National Credit Union Administration by the president of the United States. They also include his work as deputy director of the Department of Economic Research and Analysis, Office of the Comptroller of the Currency.

As soon as we had settled down to talk, Dr. Black took the conversation in a direction that I didn't expect. I had asked him, "Dr. Black, your experience in finance and government is so extensive. What is one of the most important things you've learned along the way?"

"Call me Harold, please," he began. Then he slowly leaned back in his chair. With his head cocked to one side and his fingers forming a steeple in front of him, he began to speak softly. "I have discovered that people who are considered ignorant are not—and, in fact, are a lot smarter in many ways than the people who consider themselves very intelligent. I have been asked why kids who flunk out of school and who read on a very low level can recite the words of the most complicated rap song after two listenings. And I've concluded that if you had Jay-Z rap *War and Peace*, those kids would know the story within a week. So it's not the kids who are dumb. It's the delivery system. I try to evaluate things on their own merits and on their own grounds. And I don't look down my nose at anyone."

He continued, "I try to analyze the clientele who use a particular financial product or service to learn more about these people and why they use the products they use. I don't say that someone is ignorant because they eat fish eggs or, God forbid, sushi, which I consider bait. If the fish isn't fried, I don't want to eat it. However, I don't think I'm superior because of it. Seen from another angle, fish eggs are caviar."

I quickly realized that this apparent non sequitur had a deeper point. Dr. Black is keenly interested in the choices people have—or don't have—when it comes to their finances. Among many other things, he studies how and why people borrow money.

He also studies the effects that limiting people's financial choices have on their well-being. One area of particular interest is what he sees as governments' heavy-handed attempts to protect consumers by stringently regulating interest rates. He posed a question: "When a person wants to borrow money at an interest rate that someone else considers high, should the borrower be disallowed from borrowing as a result?" He leaned forward to drive home his point. "To me, that is the ultimate snobbery. It says that someone else knows what's best for you."

One Part of the Elephant

The subject of people making judgments for others and about others is not new to Harold Black, and it has affected the way he sees the world—surprisingly, in a positive way. When asked about his personal history, he nodded his head and closed his eyes before answering. "I grew up in the South in the 1950s and 1960s. I knew Dr. Martin Luther King when he was little more than his daddy's assistant pastor and nobody knew who he was or what he would become. I came late to appreciating Martin Luther King. Having grown up in that era and participating in its events, I looked upon King as just another civil rights leader. It was only when I read Taylor Branch's *Parting the Waters* that I began to grasp his singular importance. I had always wondered why the civil rights movement did not turn into an armed conflict. In the South, we all had guns. Why didn't we use them? It was the power of King's personality and his devotion to Gandhi's nonviolent philosophy that resulted in blacks turning the other cheek.

"Having lived through the civil rights movement, I now realize that the events around me were only one part of the elephant—hopefully not the rear," he chuckled.

Well, blind man, have you seen the elephant? Tell me, what sort of thing is an elephant?

—Udana 68–69: "Parable of
the Blind Men and the Elephant"[1]

We laughed together about his reference to the parable of the blind men and the elephant. Each blind man can experience only the part of the elephant that he examines; the elephant as a whole is invisible to him. We talked about how we sometimes cling to our own limited perspectives, even when the whole elephant is standing right before us. Then he continued, "Reading more about Dr. King and that era has given me a broader view. I've given my children copies of Calvin Trillin's *An Education in Georgia*, in which my personal experiences happen to be documented."

Dr. Black's personal story is indeed an important page in the history of the civil rights movement in America, but for him it started as a simple desire to get an education. "In September of 1962, I entered the University of Georgia as one of the four first black freshmen—and the first black male student. I had just turned 17. I was put in a dorm with 600 white freshmen boys. Let's say it was an interesting experience. Growing up in the segregated South, I had never had a conversation with a white person until I arrived on the Georgia campus with my father for my application interview.

"A desegregation lawsuit had been filed against the university the previous year. In responding to the suit, the school had insisted that it never denied admission on the basis of race; instead, it simply hadn't received an application from a qualified black. We all knew that was a lie. The application form asked for your race and called for a picture—as if they didn't know the race of an applicant from Booker T. Washington High School in Atlanta. When I applied, my dad and I traveled to Athens, where we were subjected to the most amazing interview. The administrator did not shake our hands or ask us to sit down. He asked why I wanted to come to the university when I was not wanted there. He then used the 'n' word. We got up and left. Dad said, 'Well, I guess you'll have to go somewhere else.' A week later, I received a letter with a red and black border that said, 'Enclosed is your admission to the University of Georgia.' We never figured out why I was accepted.

"When we arrived at Reed Hall, where all freshman men were housed, we walked into a crowded lobby," Dr. Black continued. "It was like Moses parting the Red Sea. At the desk, the housemother said, 'You must be the Blacks.' Indeed we were. We were shown a room with a single bed. Mom said, 'Is he the *only* colored boy here?' We learned that I was. When we got back to the car, she said, 'Get in. We'll come back for your stuff, but you are not going back in there.'

"I told my mother that since I was there, I might as well stay. Dad opined that perhaps the university had accepted one black man because, after he'd been harmed or harassed, they could say they were rejecting blacks for their own safety. So I stayed. But I certainly was not made to feel welcome. The bookstore initially refused to sell me textbooks. The first time I went swimming on campus, they kicked everyone out and drained the pool. That same night, a dorm meeting was held. When I walked into the auditorium, I was determined not to sit in the back, despite those still being the 'back of the bus' days. So I walked down the aisle, with silence growing behind me. I finally picked out a row and sat down. Everyone in the row got up and moved.

"The four guys sitting directly in front of me turned around to see what the commotion was all about. They asked me, 'Are you a freshman?' When I told them I was, they said, 'Well, we are too. Can we sit with you?' These became my closest friends. They introduced me to their other friends and to Westminster House, where I could study in peace. My dorm windows were broken out literally every night, and my room was set on fire twice. Even so, my friends encountered more harassment than I did. Yet they never wavered in their friendship. That day in the auditorium, it was as if God had said, 'Harold, sit there.'

"By the way, I harbor no ill will. As a matter of fact, I'm one of Georgia's strongest supporters. I love the university. I've been on the board of directors for the College of Business and received the Distinguished Alumnus Award. I go to athletic events. It's been a great place."

Dr. Black smiled.

The Power of Making Your Own Decisions

As I absorbed Dr. Black's story, he discussed his academic background and his affection for the University of Tennessee, where he now teaches undergraduate and doctoral students about financial markets and institutions. His study of finance, coupled with his work in government, has given him a unique perspective on economics, debt, and lending in America. As we talked, Dr. Black argued for people's right—and ability—to make their own decisions. He believes that each of us should have the power to decide how and with whom we conduct financial transactions. His trust in people's common sense is palpable: "If a financial institution charges too much, people simply won't use them after a while." He observed that the unintended effect of legislation to keep interest rates low is that regulated sources of lending are squeezed out. It may seem paradoxical, but he cites numerous studies showing that removing these options actually increases overall debt and the incidence of bankruptcies. He asserts that the broader the range of borrowing options that people have to choose from, the better.

"It's not for me or you to determine what constitutes a good or bad financial decision for another person. We can only encourage more conscious choices—and honesty about those options, including both their drawbacks and their benefits."

Personal financial decisions are best made by the person whom they affect the most.

After my meeting with Dr. Black, I was even more convinced of the empowering effect of having options. His arguments confirmed my belief that personal financial decisions are best made by the person whom they affect the most. What constitutes a good or a bad financial decision is ultimately up to the individual. Any decision that is made with full awareness of the options and consequences, both for oneself and for others, is bound to bolster prosperity. We can make wise financial decisions in support of our values and dreams. To do so requires a willingness on our part to educate ourselves about our options, and then maybe to stretch a little farther. Leave judgments at the door, and don't underestimate what you—or anyone else—are capable of achieving.

The Dividing Line

Just as we don't wish to let others presume that they know what's best for us or determine our path to prosperity, we cannot presume to know what someone else's path or potential is. Senator

Leticia Van de Putte was still Leticia San Miguel and preparing for ninth grade when she realized that she was scheduled to take a home economics class. She wanted to take algebra, but in her school, the two were mutually exclusive. It had to be one or the other. On this seemingly simple decision hinged her life's path. "Girls were encouraged into home economics and otherwise guided into classes that wouldn't lead to college or professional careers. It was systemic discrimination. Right there in the ninth grade was the dividing line, where it was determined whether or not you got a higher education and became a professional. I wanted to be a pharmacist. To do that, I needed and wanted to go to college—and that required that I take algebra." Leticia asked for help. "My parents stood up for me and insisted that I be placed on the college and professional track."

Leave judgments at the door, and don't underestimate what you—or anyone else—are capable of achieving.

If she hadn't taken algebra, Leticia probably would not now be an advocate for children and education or serve as chair of the Veteran Affairs and Military Installations Committee. Nor would she have become a pharmacist and created a thriving medical center. Fortunately for the many people whom she has served, Leticia didn't settle for other people's expectations for her. She looked ahead, knew what she wanted, and worked to fulfill her goals. It was far from easy. Finishing school required hard work, and also support from her family. As she explains, "Pharmacy school was very expensive, especially the books. I got an academic scholarship, but I also took out loans, worked part time, and had family help. Everyone pitched in, including my younger sisters. In Latin culture, *quinceañera* is the celebration of a girl's fifteenth birthday. It includes a big party that many girls look forward to as a coming-out party. My sisters gave up the money that would have gone toward their parties for me."

"I always put it out there," Leticia concludes. "Sometimes I accomplished my goals and sometimes I didn't, but I always went for it. What I understood is that you must try hard no matter what." With her optimistic sights set on her future, she made good choices and she made the best of her options. When Leticia graduated from college, only eight women in her class received a pharmacology degree. Many who might have qualified had missed algebra.

A Strenuous Mountain Climb

Even young people—or perhaps especially young people—must understand their choices and the impact that their decisions, both large and small, can have on their financial welfare and potential.

I met Erin Wagner in North Carolina's state capital, Raleigh. Still in her twenties, Erin is a successful small business owner who is friendly, articulate, and engaged with her customers. She was in Raleigh to meet legislators and speak about financial lending in her state. Although she has a degree in finance, she attributes much of her expertise to growing up around her father's finance business. She says that a great deal of what she knows she learned first on her dad's knee. Erin's father obviously thought that you could never start too young. Erin agrees. Many of her clients are young people, whom she educates and advises about money matters.

"I see a lot of younger people who have fallen into substantial debt because they didn't foresee the consequences of their actions," Erin explained. "The vast majority are simply inexperienced— and just starting to figure out how to manage their income and expenses. They don't yet understand how credit works, so they fall into difficult situations unconsciously." She talked about how unconscious decisions and a lack of information are affecting many young people. "Because they don't understand their options, it makes them more susceptible to impulsive decisions. They also don't understand the outcome of those decisions—until the bills start coming. Being part of this generation, I understand where they're coming from."

Erin likened the credit scene for young people to a strenuous mountain climb. "It's like asking an inexperienced climber to scale a steep slope. A climber with experience will know what steps to take and where to plant their feet. An inexperienced climber needs a guide to help teach the discipline of the climb and point to a path with clear instructions and objectives. Education and information makes all the difference," she said. "There are many people, regardless of age, who can benefit from a conscious look at their goals and resources. When young people come into my office, we try to get them up to speed. We want to make sure they understand their choices and how to borrow appropriately and pay back their loans efficiently. We discuss the steps they can take to help them achieve their goals, or get them out of debt and establish good credit. Every decision you make matters so much, and it really helps if you make each one with real thought and planning. That's good advice for people of any age."

Doing What You Are Supposed to Do

I talked about this idea of education with Dr. Rickie Keys. As discussed earlier in the book, Rickie, like Erin, learned a great deal about finance and prosperity from a parent—in his case, at the kitchen table with his mother—and now he helps educate people who want to make more conscious financial decisions. In addition to pragmatic guidance, Rickie offers some well-founded inspiration. As you know by now, today Rickie makes educational presentations around the United States and teaches people how to achieve financial stability and success. His online programs also offer assistance with budgeting, goal achievement, and prosperity growth.

Rickie teaches these concepts through his organization, Renewal Financial.[2] "Financial education is critically important. If you didn't learn financial skills at the kitchen table, it is vital that you learn them now." He argues that people can make good financial decisions when they have the information they need and when they understand what it takes to achieve their financial goals. Being able to anticipate potential obstacles and roadblocks can also prepare people to either handle or avoid them. "For advisors, it's important to educate and not just tell people what to do," he says. "Once people understand their options, they know how to choose what's right for them. Understanding their protections as consumers is also hugely beneficial."

Even young people—or perhaps especially young people— must understand their choices and the impact that decisions, both large and small, can have on their financial welfare and potential.

The Kids Are Gonna Be All Right

Groups of teenagers are making their way to their next classroom. The kids' personal styles and appearance run the gamut from straitlaced and button-down to hipsters with tattoos. All wear their attitude like a coat of armor. You might be tempted to guess which ones will succeed in life and which will take a less than stellar trajectory. Of course, it's impossible to tell from appearances.

And the determining factor can be something as simple as having a role model or reading an inspiring how-to book—and this is true at any age. Looking to wise people who have blazed a path to prosperity before us is a time-honored and powerful way to educate ourselves and contribute to our own psychology of wealth.

The kids in the hall have just been given a book that, if its message is taken to heart, will help them make good choices. The book is *SUCCESS for Teens*,[3] provided by Stuart Johnson, owner of *SUCCESS* magazine, who created a foundation to help kids develop life skills. Leah McCann, director of development for the SUCCESS Foundation, explained, "When Stuart was a teen, he was given a book called *The Magic of Thinking Big*, by David J. Schwartz. That book inspired him and spurred his own personal development. It helped him understand that the first step in taking on the challenges of business and life is to work on oneself. He wants to share that experience with the next generation, so we're reaching out with book donations to youth organizations to support and inspire kids to set goals, build dreams, and create high self-esteem."

KEEP YOUR GOALS IN PLAIN VIEW

Write down five things you want in your life.
Examples:

1. A new car

2. The love of my life

3. To fulfill my life's purpose

4. A great job

5. A new home

Post this where you will see it every day!

Stuart Johnson says, "I think it's important—and not only for kids—to recognize that there's no one definition for success. And each choice you make can add up to a big difference, whether you live in the projects or in the nicest neighborhood in town."

Whether our teen years are recently behind us or a distant speck in the rearview mirror, it is never too early or too late to develop a psychology of wealth.

The little things you do every day, whether positive or negative, will determine what kind of life you lead.[4]

—Stuart Johnson

Home for the Holidays

There is one more part of Tony Cupisz's story that I want to share with you. You may recall that Tony and his twin brother, Mike, are two of the four co-founders of a successful multinational company, and that early in their lives, they were abandoned on the steps of a trailer with their sister, Annette. When Tony and Mike were adopted by family acquaintances and their sister was taken in by a relative of their mother, the adoptive families agreed that the two boys would not see their sister again until they reached 18.

"When we turned 18," Tony said, "we met nearly everybody in our biological mother's family, including our grandfather. Everyone appeared extremely happy to see us. Mike and I wondered, 'Who are all these people?' But we were something to them; we were the kids they hadn't seen since we were two years old. When we saw our sister, we all just stared at each other. Then, within five minutes, we felt like we'd known each other our whole lives."

Tony and Mike immediately started to learn more about their family, including their father. "Annette knew that our biological father's name was Tony Aquino. So the first thing we did was look in the phone book for Aquinos—just out of curiosity. A few weeks later, Mike was working out at the gym with a friend, who happened to be Italian. Mike said, 'Hey, I just found out that I'm Italian, like you.' The friend replied, 'How did you figure that out?' Mike explained that we'd recently been reunited with our sister, and that she'd told us our biological father's last name was Aquino. The friend quickly replied that he knew someone named *Tony* Aquino. He had recently bought a car from him.

"So in the excitement of the moment, Mike and the friend hopped in the car and drove directly to the car dealership. When they walked in, they asked the first salesperson they saw if a Tony Aquino worked there. Now, they were just out of the gym—pumped up and sweaty and wearing ripped T-shirts. The man thought they must be disgruntled customers looking for some trouble. So he said, 'No, no, there's no Tony Aquino here. He doesn't work here anymore, and I don't know anything about his whereabouts.' As they walked away, the man asked why they were looking for him. Mike replied, 'He might be my father.' And then Mike and his friend drove away."

The salesperson happened to be a good friend of Tony Aquino, and he had recognized Mike's friend from his recent purchase of a car. So he dug out the friend's car loan application to find his name and phone number and passed the information to Tony Aquino.

"Later that evening, Tony Aquino called our house," Tony continued. "At first, we thought he was our friend playing a joke. So the very first thing Mike and I did was to swear at him!" Tony laughed. "'Who is this? Come on, stop messing with us!' But then our father said, 'No, honestly. It's me. It's your father.

You've been looking for me.' As we started to realize it was true, we began to ask each other questions—things like, 'How tall are you? What do you look like?' After we had talked awhile, we set a time to go to his house. And so we met our biological father for the first time.

"Well, I can tell you, we discovered a couple of interesting things," Tony said. "For one, he had lived within a mile of us most of our lives. Meeting him was surreal. We were very inquisitive. We wanted to discover who he was, to ask him questions and build a relationship. So we did, and we compared everything—our baby toes, our personalities, our builds. We connected with him and laughed right away. We liked each other immediately."

When asked whether he and Mike felt angry with their biological father, Tony said, "No, not at all. We just accepted that whatever had happened had happened. We were unhappy with our upbringing, so when we met him, we did think, 'God, it would have been so much better if we'd been with him.' So we did feel a void—and wondered how it could have been. But we weren't mad at anyone. We felt no resentment or blame. The first thing we noticed when we met people on both sides of the family was that many of them offered excuses about why they couldn't take us when we were young. But Mike and I never asked. We would look at each other, knowing it didn't really matter. We just thought, 'We're meeting you today. We're not interested in the past. We're just interested in getting to know you now.'"

As Tony got to know the Aquino family, he noticed a family trait that had nothing to do with size, height, or looks. It was an important inner quality. "My brother, my sister, and everyone in the Aquino family tree has a good heart, an innocence, and a curiosity—almost a childlike mindset. Truly good hearts. We're shocked when someone does something that isn't right—for example, if someone lies to us," Tony said.

"When Mike and I grew up, we always felt like outcasts. We felt like we irritated our adoptive parents. Even if they loved us, it seemed that they didn't *like* us.

"After we reconnected, my sister Annette would come over to visit Mike and me, to see us and the Cupisz family, and to be with us during the holidays. Then, as soon as we could, Annette, Mike, and I would make an excuse, jump in the car, and go to our biological father's house to spend a few hours with him and his family. My father was remarried and had young kids, and we enjoyed visiting with them all.

"We felt better there than we ever felt anywhere else," Tony explained. "And we didn't really know why; it just felt right. I remember one Christmas dinner. We all were sitting around the table, and I realized everybody was the same! We were all loud, obnoxious, and animated," Tony laughed. "Mike and I had been goofy kids. We would do skits and act weird. And there we were with my biological father, and he was doing the same thing—and all of us, the kids and us, were all acting the same way. It was hilarious. And I remember sitting there thinking, 'Oh my gosh, this is where we came from. This is where we feel we belong.' We had never really connected with our adoptive parents that way. And here we connected instantly."

JUST START MOVING

Take advantage of what is available now. Although it may not be exactly what you believe you want, it might be a step onto the path to your dreams. Just keep moving in the right direction.

Another quality was also shared at that table. Tony realized, "My dad was the same as us in another way. He had the same drive within him that we did. He was a dreamer and wanted more. He had the feeling—the spirit—of believing you can be better and of striving for something better. Somehow that had passed through to us."

Tony had not been raised with the financial advantages or emotionally wealthy environment of some of his successful peers. His adoptive parents had not expected much of him. Yet today the success that Tony and his brother Mike have achieved is acknowledged with pride by their families on all sides—and they are an inspiration to thousands.

Tony had found something in his own character that allowed him to overcome his early disadvantages, an intangible quality that is at the core of his being—proof that if we follow our hearts, even the most improbable beginnings can lead to full and prosperous lives.

The Whole Elephant

As I drove away from Dr. Harold Black's office, I thought about his metaphor of the elephant. For me, writing this book has been a way to try to see the "whole elephant" of prosperity— not just the parts that are visible from my individual perspective and experience. The image of the elephant reminds us to recognize that we can't necessarily see the big picture from our own point of view. An elephant is a magnificent, if unlikely, creature. I was grateful for the opportunities I'd had to step back and get a glimpse. Through dialogues and discourses, I had come to a more complete understanding of the countless paths to prosperity and the rich nature of the psychology of wealth. I also remembered that in many cultures, the image of an elephant with an upturned trunk represents the removal of all obstacles. I knew that whatever obstacles may appear in our way, remembering the big picture—where we want to go and the power of trusting in our ability to get there—will help see us through. Doing so will allow us to embrace the tremendous possibilities for ourselves, our families, and our communities—and experience our highest potential for prosperity.

Based on my discussions with many successful people, I have learned that having a healthy psychology of wealth means taking responsibility for one's own decisions. As I talked with Rickie Keys, Dr. Harold Black, and Erin Wagner, another facet of this psychology emerged clearly—that is, to make the most beneficial decisions and to chart the best possible financial course, we must also take responsibility for educating ourselves. Part of conscious financial living and creating prosperity is seeking out knowledge about our options and resources. Put simply, it is learning how money works. We must make ourselves the most capable decision makers we can be. To do this, we can learn from our parents, teachers, mentors, and truly qualified advisors, or simply through reading, talking with, and listening to the best sources we can find. This education will not only serve us; it will expand us. And then, when we have added our own experience to this education, we in turn can pass this wisdom to others, including to the next generation.

A wealth psychology is not a particular financial strategy or method. Nor is it an inner determination to obtain riches or fulfill one's monetary dreams or desires. Prosperity is not defined by how much money we have accumulated or how little debt we have. The psychology of wealth is a simple and pragmatic call to nurture the qualities and attitudes within ourselves that will create a prosperous life. This suggests a commitment to bring more consciousness to all our decisions, large and small. It asks us to discover what is most meaningful to us as individuals and to become aware of how each decision and action moves us either toward those values or away from them.

Having a wealth psychology means that we feel grateful for what we have and acknowledge what we've accomplished. We know that generosity toward others is abundance in motion, and that giving creates more abundance in us. With this psychology, we accept that we're responsible for what we create, no matter what life may provide or remove along the way. We expect the best of ourselves, and we recognize that the golden path to true prosperity, to a life of happiness and fulfillment, begins by showing up and putting one foot in front of the other.

Notes

CHAPTER 1

1. Senator Van de Putte served as cochair of the 2008 Democratic National Convention, and is a strong advocate for children, veterans, and high-quality public education. She currently serves as chair of the Veteran Affairs and Military Installations Committee and as a member of the Senate Committees on Education, State Affairs, and Business and Commerce. She is the incoming president pro tem of the Texas State Senate.

2. Shanna Hogan, "Lottery's Lucky Losers," *Times Publications*, September 2008.

3. "From Porsches to Bankruptcy," *Arizona Republic*, July 16, 2006.

4. Hogan, "Lottery's Lucky Losers."

5. David Fusaro, "Lottery Winnings: Easy Money That's Hard to Handle," Columbia News Service, February 13, 2007.

6. Renewal Financial Services, LLC, http://www.renewalfinancial.com/news.

7. Robert M. Williams, *PSYCH-K . . . The Missing Peace in Your Life!* (Crestone, Colo.: Myrddin Publications, 2004).

CHAPTER 2

1. Walter Coffey, "The Panic of 1819: The First Major Depression in U.S. History Sets Many Economic Trends," *Suite 101*, February 21, 2010, http://www.suite101.com/content/the-panic-of-1819-a204503.

2. Wendell Cox, "Root Causes of the Financial Crisis: A Primer," October 28, 2008, http://www.newgeography.com.

3. Rana Foroohar, "Keeping Economics Real," *Newsweek*, October 17, 2008.

4. "History of the Sewing Machine," Museum of American Heritage. http://www.moah.org/.

5. Georgia Lund, "How the Sewing Machine Made Credit Cards Possible," http://www.associatedcontent.com/article/467260/how_the_sewing_machine_made_credit.html?cat=3, Dec. 7, 2007.

6. "Installment Buying, Selling, and Financing,"accessed October 8, 2011, http://www.answers.com/topic/installment-buying-selling-and-financing.

7. Donncha Marron, *Consumer Credit in the United States: A Sociological Perspective from the 19th Century to the Present* (New York: Palgrave MacMillan, 2009), 38–48.

8. Sammy Kicklighter, Brevard Piano, http://www.brevardpiano.com/.

9. "Marketing History of the Piano," last modified February 4, 2010, http://www.cantos.org/Piano/History/marketing.html.

10. "The Advertising of Installment Plans," Oakwood Publishing Company, http://www.studyworld.com/newsite/reportessay/science/Technical%5CThe_Advertising_of_Installment_Plans-3485143.htm.

11. "Henry Ford Changes the World, 1908," Eyewitness to History, 2005, http://www.eyewitnesstohistory.com.

12. Claire Suddath, "A Brief History of the Middle Class," *Time*, February 27, 2009.

13. Ibid.

14. Frank Jordans, "USA Comes Up a Bit Short in Global Better Life Index," *USA Today*, May 24, 2011, http://www.usatoday.com/money/world/2011-05-24-oecd-better-life-index_n.html.

15. Susan Page, "Western Cities Fare Best in Well-Being Index," *USA Today*, February 15, 2010, http://www.usatoday.com/news/nation/2010-02-15-cities_N.html.

CHAPTER 3

1. Thomas J. Stanley and William D. Danko, *The Millionaire Next Door: The Surprising Secrets of America's Wealthy* (New York: Pocket Books, 1998).

2. Amy Chua, *Battle Hymn of the Tiger Mother* (New York: Penguin Press, 2011).

3. Darren Hardy, "27 Resources for Your Success," a list of essential tools and technologies to help achievers gain the competitive edge, http://darrenhardy.success.com/2008/07/27-resources-to-accelerate-your-success-some-might-surprise-you/.

4. Donald J. Trump and Bill Zanker, *Think Big and Kick Ass in Business and Life* (New York: HarperCollins, 2007), 11.

5. Donald J. Trump and Robert T. Kiyosaki, *Why We Want You to Be Rich: Two Men—One Message* (Phoenix, Ariz.: Rich Press, 2008), 101.

6. Donald J. Trump, *Think Like a Champion: An Informal Education in Business and Life* (New York: Vanguard Press, 2009), 28.

7. Henry Ford; http://allpoetry.com/quote/by/Henry%20Ford.

CHAPTER 4

1. Charles Paikert, "With Szifra Birke of Lexington Wealth Management Inc.," August 13, 2007, http://www.investmentnews.com/article/20070813/FREE/70813028.

2. Nathaniel Branden, "The Power of Positive Self Esteem," reprinted from *Bottom Line/Personal* 15, no. 11, 6-1-94, 1991.

3. Robert Reasoner, "Counseling Connection," National Association for Self-Esteem, http://www.self-esteem-nase.org/.

4. Glen H. Elder and Rand D. Conger, *Children of the Land: Adversity and Success in Rural America* (Chicago: University of Chicago Press, 2000).

5. Donald J. Trump and Bill Zanker, *Think Big and Kick Ass in Business and Life* (New York: HarperCollins, 2007), 41, 44.

6. Darren Hardy, *The Compound Effect: Multiplying Your Success, One Simple Step at a Time* (Lake Dallas, Tex.: SUCCESS Books, 2010).

CHAPTER 5

1. Darren Hardy, *The Compound Effect: Multiplying Your Success, One Simple Step at a Time* (Lake Dallas, Tex.: SUCCESS Books, 2010).

2. Brian Tracy, "Taking Personal Responsibility," http://www.successmethods.org/brian_tracy-a19.html.

3. Ibid.

4. "A Cherokee Legend," http://www.firstpeople.us/FP-Html-Legends/Two Wolves-Cherokee.html.

5. Paul G. Durbin, Ph.D., "A Tribute to Viktor Frankl,"1986, http://www.infinityinst.com/articles/trib_vik_frankl.html.

6. Louis Hyman, *Debtor Nation* (Princeton, N.J.: Princeton University Press, 2011), p. 150.

7. José D. Roncal, "Consumer Debt in the U.S.," September 1, 2008, http://www.financialspeculation.com/attachments/consumer-debt.pdf, 23.

8. Ibid., 24–29.

9. Norman Vincent Peale, http://quotationsbook.com/quote/684/.

CHAPTER 6

1. Tim Ogle, "Value for Money More Important than Low Price, Say Shoppers," January 11, 2011, http://www.talkingretail.com/news/industry-news/value-for-money-more-important-than-low-price-say-shoppers.

2. Melissa Koide and Rachel Schneider, "How Should We Serve the Short-Term Credit Needs of Low-Income Consumers?" Joint Center for Housing

Studies, Harvard University, August 2010. Paper originally presented at Moving Forward: The Future of Consumer Credit and Mortgage Finance, a national symposium held on February 18 and 19, 2010, at Harvard Business School in Boston, Massachusetts.

3. William Baldwin, "The Investment Guide 2011," *Forbes*, June 27, 2011, 68.

4. Kevin Wack, "For Banks, Little Progress on Loans to the Unbanked," *American Banker*, September 22, 2011.

5. Lendol Calder, *Financing the American Dream: A Cultural History of Consumer Credit* (Princeton, N.J.: Princeton University Press, 1999), 301–302.

6. Ibid, p. 302.

7. Rep. Johnny Shaw, D-Bolivar, District 80—Hardeman and part of Madison Counties. District address: P.O. Box 191, 123 West Market Street, Bolivar, TN 38008; rep.johnny.shaw@capitol.tn.gov.

8. Jacque Hillman and Jimmy Hart, "Tent City, October 1960: Fayette, Haywood County Blacks Forced from Their Homes for Trying to Exercise Right to Vote," *Jackson Sun* Special Report, 2003.

CHAPTER 7

1. Claire Suddath, "A Brief History of the Middle Class," *Time*, February 27, 2009.

2. Ibid.

3. "Buy Now, Pay Later: A History of Personal Credit," Exhibition organized by Baker Library Historical Collections, Harvard Business School, October 22, 2010–June 3, 2011.

4. Cornelius Frolik, "Residents Forgoing Dental Care to Save Money," *Dayton Daily News*, July 6, 2011.

5. For more information about Jeff Burch's work with military and federal employees, see Jeff Burch, *Survival Tactics: Money Book* and *Military: Money Book* (Sheridan Books, 2011) and http://moneymattersusa.org/.

CHAPTER 8

1. Constance Rosenblum, "'Hetty': Scrooge in Hoboken," *New York Times*, December 19, 2004.

2. Yisrael Nathan, "The Kindness That Came Back," *Jewish Magazine*, November 1997, http://www.inspirationalstories.com/4/403.html.

CHAPTER 9

1. Michael Stern, D.C., founder of Research for Alternative Medicine (RAM) Foundation, has pioneered new chiropractic methodologies and facilitates chiropractic seminars; http//drmstern@gmail.com, http://chiropractictension

release.com/. See also Larry Trivieri, *The American Holistic Medical Association Guide to Holistic Health* (New York: Wiley, 2001) and Larry Trivieri, John W. Anderson, and Burton Goldberg Group, *Alternative Medicine: The Definitive Guide* (Berkeley, Calif.: Celestial Arts, 2002).

2. Denise Fast, http://denisefastpoetry.com.

3. Jalal al-Din Rumi, *It Is What It Is: The Personal Discourses of Rumi,* trans. and ed. Doug Marman (Ridgefield, Wash.: Spiritual Dialogues Project, 2010).

CHAPTER 10

1. Georgia Firefighters Burn Foundation, 2575 Chantilly Dr., Atlanta, GA 30324, (404) 320-6223, www.gfbf.org, contact@gfbf.org. "Helping burn survivors in their journey of recovery as well as to prevent others from experiencing the traumatic event of a burn injury."

2. Camp Oo-U-La. Camp Oo-U-La welcomes children between the ages of seven and seventeen who have suffered serious burns. For one week, children come together free of charge for camp in Winder, Georgia. Contact Resource Development Coordinator, Georgia Firefighters Burn Foundation, (405) 320-6223.

3. Oprah Winfrey, "What I Know for Sure," *O, The Oprah Magazine* 11, no. 11 (November 2010), 236.

4. Ibid.

CHAPTER 11

1. Udana 68–69: "Parable of the Blind Men and the Elephant," provided by Randy Wang, http://www.cs.princeton.edu/~rywang/berkeley/258/parable.html.

2. Rickie C. Keys, Ph.D., MPH, Senior Fellow, CAAP, Renewal Financial Services, LLC, "A Fresh Start," http://www.renewalfinancial.com/.

3. Editors of the SUCCESS Foundation, *SUCCESS for Teens.* The SUCCESS Foundation can be reached at (940) 497-9700, info@SuccessFoundation.org. The advisory board includes Donald Trump, Robert and Kim Kiyosaki, Stedman Graham, Paul Zane Pilzer, Darren Hardy, Jeff Olson, John Addison, and Greg Provenzano.

4. Ibid.

Book Club Questions

1. A psychology of wealth can be learned in childhood through the values we are taught. Senator Leticia Van de Putte recounted important lessons that she learned from her parents. Discuss how her parents helped to prepare her for a future she didn't expect.

2. If you were to define the word *wealth* right now, what words would you use? How might these words help you to better understand your personal psychology of wealth?

3. Tony Cupisz and his twin brother, Mike, had a difficult childhood. Ultimately they realized they could create a life that was different from the life of their adoptive parents. What were some actions Tony took to start moving toward his goals? How might you apply some of his strategies to move toward greater success and happiness?

4. Self-esteem is a fundamental human need. When we have a solid sense of self-esteem, we feel confident in our ability to cope with life's challenges. Why is self-esteem an essential component of a psychology of wealth?

5. Our lives reflect the conscious and unconscious choices that we make each day. Darren Hardy of *SUCCESS* magazine observed, "In essence, you make your choices, and then your

choices make you. Every decision, no matter how slight, alters the trajectory of your life." What slight changes might you make each day to affect your life positively, both now and in the future?

6. Viktor Frankl, a Nazi concentration camp survivor, became known for teaching that life's meaning comes not from what happens to us, but from how we respond to it. Discuss the difference between reacting and responding consciously to what life presents to us.

7. Traditional consumer installment lending is still done face to face, the old-fashioned way. All borrowing once required face-to-face discussions between the borrower and the lender about the borrower's needs and means. How did so much of our borrowing morph from a transaction that requires consultation and deliberation into the ability to borrow and spend instantaneously? Discuss how this change has enhanced or detracted from your psychology of wealth.

8. What would our world look like today if credit had never been extended to average citizens?

9. During the recession, many people have become afraid to spend and borrow. Why is this fear counterproductive, both to us as individuals and to our society?

10. One of the joys of experiencing prosperity is the ability to give back—to take care of ourselves so well that we can afford to share with others abundantly. How does giving open us to receiving even more?

11. Dennis Gardin turned the worst experience of his life into the greatest blessing. What did he learn by overcoming his fear, and what can we learn from him about the psychology of wealth?

Index

About the Author

Charles Richards, Ph.D., is a Doctor of Clinical Psychology, author and licensed psychotherapist in private practice in San Diego, California. He has developed and refined an innovative and highly effective therapeutic process that allows clients to achieve greater health in all areas of their lives. For more than 10 years, he also trained and coached senior executives of Fortune 100 corporations in management and leadership skills at the Center for Creative Leadership, La Jolla. His clients at CCL have included General Motors, IBM, Motorola, QUALCOMM, Sony, Apple, Whirlpool, Honda, SAP, and other well-known companies. He is also an internationally known speaker and presenter.